YOU CAN'T FILLET A NIBBLE...

IT'S THE CATCH THAT COUNTS

By Gary Coxe

Gary Coxe © 2013

ISBN-10: 0615800254
ISBN-13: 978-0-6158002-5-7

Published by Coxe Enterprises.
www.GaryCoxe.com

Edited by Jennifer-Crystal Johnson
www.jennifercrystaljohnson.com

Table of Contents

Chapter One
You Can't Fillet a Nibble... You Can Only Fillet the Catch!   5
Chapter Two
Getting Beyond the Nibble   11
Chapter Three
The Three Key Ingredients to Mastering Persistence   19
Chapter Four
The Real Difference Between Being Passive or Persistent   33
Chapter Five
Are You Smart or Stupid? Marketing 101   39
Chapter Six
The Mindset of True Persistence   61
Chapter Seven
Lay Down the Law: "You can't handle the truth!"   71
About the Author   82

Chapter One
You Can't Fillet a Nibble...
You Can Only Fillet the Catch!

I once hired someone to help manage my sales team who thought it would be an easy job. It was very evident in a very short time that he wasn't really fit for this position. He was also responsible for his own sales while managing.

In tracking the numbers, he could tell that I wasn't very happy with his progress. As we communicated I'd ask him how things were going. I would often get this message of false hope from him that, "this company was interested and this other company as well. We'll know in a day or two about this other one." After hearing this without results for weeks, I came up with the expression, "You can't fillet a nibble!"

Yes, it's exciting to think about the possible bite or catch, but nibbles can get you excited only for so long. Without a bite and a true catch with the fish in the boat, you're going to starve. This person tried to give me false hope by getting me excited about the 'nibbles' that never bit and converted to real catches or sales.

Don't get me wrong here. Nibbles are exciting and they have their place in keeping us motivated and giving us hope, but you can't fillet a nibble; you can only fillet the catch. Nibbles don't count on your bottom line. Can you imagine looking at a company's profit and loss statement and seeing a section for nibbles or possible sales? How ludicrous would that be... not to mention quite humorous.

As I just mentioned, nibbles are exciting and do have their place in sales. For example, I often keep a list of companies I call a 'Nibble List' that we use when we have companies that show an interest in working with us. This list is more to enable us to focus on the specific companies that have shown some interest in working with my company. Then we make an extra effort to 'pull' them in and go beyond just the nibble. It also gives everyone hope for possible future business. Your future is your present. If you have lots of hope in your future, your present will be exciting.

It's like throwing out a fishing line and getting a nibble. You pull the line in and the fish seems to hang on so you reel in more and you lose the fish. You throw in your line again and the same thing happens. Now you're really getting excited. There's a good chance you're not going to change your location because the fish are biting right where you're at. A nibble at least is better than nothing, not to mention it at least gives you an indication you're getting closer to your objective.

How to Have the Guts of a Burglar

So let's move our attention over to you now. Are you getting average results... or less than average results? Or maybe you're going through this material with me because you *want* above average results. If so, perhaps you need to create the persistent mindset of a millionaire. One of my goals is to show you how to have more guts. Yes, like the guts of a burglar.

You can accomplish a lot when you have the guts of a burglar! What does this really mean, though? This idea or concept of having the guts of a burglar first came to me years ago, early in my career, when I had the opportunity to share the stage with Business Philosopher Jim Rhon in Tampa, Florida.

Jim had had a prior event the night before in Chicago. There were no more commercial flights to Tampa that evening to get him back in time for our event in the morning. Being an avid aviation fan and pilot, I offered my services to the promoter and personally flew up to Chicago that evening to get him back in time for the seminar.

This was the first of many times getting to meet Jim. One of the conversations we had while flying together before he fell asleep to get some rest was about success. He shared with me examples of people who have the "guts of a burglar" and how it helped them to succeed. His point was if you're fearless and have the guts of a burglar, you do things and get results far beyond those of the average person.

I thought about this concept for some time after that. I would regularly ask myself, "Do I really have the guts of a burglar?" I felt like I did but I wanted more of it. I worked harder and harder to be more consistent and persistent toward my goals. I became more and more fearless. I wanted to regularly have the guts of a burglar. It's one of the best ways I know how to get beyond average results.

A burglar doesn't stop until he gets what he wants. Nothing gets in his way. When an obstacle presents itself, he goes through it, under it, around it, over of it, whatever it takes.

How often do you have such drive and persistence toward a goal or project? How quickly do you give up or give in? Or do you simply keep going? Do you have a high or low tolerance to emotional pain? If it's low, you'll cave under pressure. When you have the guts of a burglar, you thrive on overcoming challenges and obstacles... you actually get addicted to it. Imagine that, being addicted to challenges, obstacles, and problems!

How addicted are you to fighting for your goals and dreams... especially during the challenging times when all odds seem to be against you? Do you get an adrenaline rush when you wake up each morning to tackle them? Do you have that rush even when you're down and out? Imagine being that way each morning and what that would do in helping you have more drive and sustainability toward reaching and attaining your goals?

It's my objective to share with you some tools to make that happen for you in your own pursuits. If you've never met me or don't know my story you'll soon see why people recognize me as one of the most persistent people that you will ever meet in your life. I'm going to share with you how I got to have the guts of a burglar and how you can, too. The rewards are often greater than you think. Financially for me, it's made me millions and opened doors that I would have never dreamed of.

I'm going to take you on journey of the persistent mindset of a millionaire. You'll learn how to think differently so that nothing – and I mean *nothing* – can stop you. This will be the most in-depth book I believe you'll read on this subject. It will give you so much clarity on how to be incredibly unstoppable. I hope you're going to love what you read.

I'm *not* going to just simply tell you, "The more no's you get the closer to a yes you are." You already know that. That's common sense. But knowing this doesn't make a switch turn on in someone's head if they have a problem with making more calls or handling more no's. So it takes more understanding to get this concept.

I'm not here to tell you that you need to be more persistent. Duh, everyone knows that's important. More importantly, I'm going to show you how to train your brain to make this happen so you, too, will have the guts of a burglar like I do. You'll get far more results.

Most people would agree that if they were more persistent in certain areas in their lives they'd get more results. What many people *don't* know is *why* they are not more persistent even if they see the need to be. You'll find that answer and many more as you continue reading.

I'll share with you examples of how I have relentlessly pursued corporate accounts for up to a decade before getting results. I've texted some people 20 or 30 times where most would stop at two or three attempts. How many years do you pursue your goals? How many times will you attempt to try to contact someone? When might you quit? I'll take you into my thought process that makes me totally mentally unstoppable and reaps incredible results. You'll be able to do the same.

I'll show you how to take the most ticked off potential client and turn them around so that they are putty in your hands. I'll show you how to turn them around so much they'll only be able to describe you as someone with 'class' and become a raving fan of yours. When last have you had a customer describe you or your company as someone with class? Not a bad description to have, is it?

One client, after I called him continually for four years, finally let me in to speak to his organization. Why? He said he wanted his team to develop my unstoppable, persistent mindset and attitude. He also wanted to know what I have that would cause me to call month after month, year after year, and every time I spoke to him I was as nice to him as the first time I called.

Trust me when I tell you this: this is a *mindset*. You must *become it*. You can't just be persistent, you must become it. This isn't through positive thinking rah-rah stuff. This is down and dirty, getting in the trenches, let's-make-things-happen-and-take-action material. It's a mindset that you must learn to master if you desire more results without white-knuckling it.

At first you may have to force some of the behaviors and habits that I will share with you, but once you see the results, your thought process will begin to shift as this new way of thinking becomes second nature and natural.

I'm going to help you determine how to know how many times to call a potential client or customer. Should you leave a message or not? When should you call back? How should you deal with thoughts that you might be bothering them or contacting them too much?

After reading this book you will immediately need to put these strategies to work. The more you apply, the more results you will achieve. You will be amazed how your life, sales, and finances can change.

I won't bore you about me too much but I'll give you a brief background about myself if you're not familiar with it. I started my career as an entrepreneur with my first business at age 11 and my second business at age 15. When I was younger, macramé was a big thing and I used to sell macramé key chains to my friends.

Then at 15 I got into making and repairing jewelry until, just a few years later, I had my own wholesale and retail fine jewelry manufacturing facility. I was my family's first generation master jeweler. At such a young age, every obstacle was against me. I came out on top, making over $100,000 a year as a teenager.

I did have a great advantage starting my business at such an early age. It was that I was too young to know better. When you're young you have a tendency at times to take more risk than you might when you are an adult. I didn't know what I didn't know. What other people say about you may also not bother you as much when you're a fearless, naive teenager.

If we're not careful we let worry about others' opinions rent space in our heads and we allow all that junk to slow us down or even cause us to want to quit. I've been there, and it's not a great feeling. Lack of results as you work toward your goals will give this feeling to you more often than not. As you work toward your goals over the next few days, stop and think about what you'd do and how you'd react to things differently if you had more guts! Yes, the guts of a burglar.

I have learned that if you are passive, you will be poorer. Keep in mind that making $50,000 a year is poor*er* than someone making $100,000 a year. Making $100,000 a year is poor*er* than someone making $200,000 a year, and so on. When you have this book completed, you'll see the distinct difference between being passive and being persistent. Being passive will make you poorer while being persistent will make you prosperous and wealthy. There are some negative side effects to being persistent which I'll share with you, but you'll also soon agree the benefits far outweigh the side effects of being passive.

It's time now to get into the persistent mindset of a millionaire. Let's begin.

Chapter Two
Getting Beyond the Nibble

It goes without saying how important leads are to making sales. Without leads you have no potential for making the sales. There is, however, a huge danger in working your leads. It's called "irrational optimism," or simply having false hope.

"Sales" in and of itself is not always easy. And often, especially people who are new to sales, will get a false sense of success or security because they have many leads that are "biting" or "nibbling." But we must never forget that you *cannot fillet a nibble*. Like fishing, the ultimate goal is the catch, not the nibble. Yes, after throwing in the line the next step is to get the nibble. But what's better, five thousand nibbles in the water or one fish in the boat?

What's better, five thousand nibbles in the water or one fish in the boat?

We all have the natural tendency to look for hope. It's a good thing. Nibbles give us hope. They get us excited. That's why we like them. Not to mention, as crazy as it sounds, nibbles help us justify feeling good when we're not making any sales because we have the possibility or hope of future sales. It doesn't take long for that feeling to crash if no catches are made. But if we are not careful they can also give us false hope. If you don't have the right hook or bait, you may end up with nibbles all day long and nothing in the boat. It won't take long to lose all of your excitement.

After a while, if you're serious about your fishing, nibbles are not enough for you. It's not the end result we are looking for. They do, however, keep us going and excited, at least for the moment, but if that's all we're getting, we're wasting time. Don't lose precious time getting excited over false hope. Determine what can be done better to hook the fish and get them into the boat. That's what counts, especially if you're hungry and you have no other source of food.

The Emotional Danger Nibbles Cause

There is a grave danger that's caused by nibbles. I believe it is also one of the reasons people quit in business and sales. Watch any kid as he gets excited with a nibble while fishing. It's the most amazing experience for him. Especially if it's his first experience. But let's say that, for hours, all this kid is getting are nibbles while people beside him do better by catching fish and are watching him only get nibbles. This poor kid is going to start feeling so bad because he's going to think that maybe there is something wrong with him. "Why is everyone else catching something and I'm not?" he starts reasoning. He goes from an incredible high about getting the nibbles to an incredible low about not catching anything because he's the only one not being successful.

It's hard from time to time not to get too excited over a great nibble, especially if you lose the catch right before you get it to the boat; but if you're not careful, the emotional fall from the high of the nibble to the low of not getting a catch can wipe people out in sales. I see it all the time. People new to sales are very prone to this.

Because they lack experience, they will get so excited over small things that an experienced person wouldn't even look at twice. Just because a number of people have shown interest in their product or opportunity isn't enough to excite an old pro. And more often than not, a newbie's perception of someone showing interest is often distorted because they are looking for the emotional high that comes with a nibble.

It's quite amazing how soon that exciting nibble turns into discouragement or causes some people to quit because they realize that they can't fillet a nibble and there will be no way to pay the bills that way.

I've seen people fool themselves into thinking certain people they've spoken to are really interested in what they have to offer when in fact they really are not. The other person they talked to just couldn't tell them no and perhaps took their business card and gave them their number.

For many people who are new in sales that's really exciting and a huge nibble. But sooner or later they will find out they can't get ahold of that person as the 'nibble' of a contact is now dodging their calls or not picking up the phone. And there goes the emotional roller coaster again.

It's this extreme high of a nibble to the extreme low of not converting it to a sale that will lead most newbies to run away and quit.

My sales team is very focused on keeping track of numbers. We make it a point to track how many outbound calls are made each day and for the week. It is so easy to get tempted to focus on those numbers. It's exciting to see how many calls are made and watch them increase on a regular basis. But we have to always keep reminding ourselves that this is not the bottom line. Making lots of calls and contacts is great but that doesn't pay the bills. The catch is what adds to the bottom line.

It's also important to balance our thinking to come to realize that if we don't get any nibbles that it might be time to move to another spot completely. So nibbles aren't – by themselves – a bad thing. They do give us hope. But too much false hope can be a huge let-down when we don't get results.

In one of our marking campaigns our team used to keep what we called our "whale" board. That's a list similar to the one I shared with you in the previous chapter. We had specific definitions or criteria for each. For a company to be placed on our nibble board we had to have at least made verbal contact with them and they had to have seemed interested in our services by being willing to accept more of our marketing materials or by asking pertinent questions.

The whale board was different. In Vegas they refer to whales as people who do some high dollar gambling, up into the hundreds of thousands or millions of dollars. Only specific large companies could qualify to even get onto the whale board. But first, contact had to be made and more than the usual interest had to be shown to us. That would include perhaps a scheduled phone meeting or a showcase presentation for the CEO and other leaders.

One of our goals was to have as many qualified companies on these boards as possible. Why? It gave us hope. Just like that nibble from the fish gives hope, so do these boards. We knew, though, that the board only represented hope. Not a contract or sale, but it was certainly a start. When someone made more contact or added a company to the board, we'd all soon find out about it because it gave the entire team hope as well. Never forget that hope is the anchor to the soul.

Just make sure you're riding on *real* hope as false hope is fleeting.

Not to sound as if I'm contradicting myself, though. Temporary false hope, which a nibble might be categorized as, isn't always that bad. Why is that, you might ask? Hope gives you a future, even false hope will do that for us. That's why the initial nibbles are exciting. They give us hope, whether it's true or false; you have hope of something good that could, will, or might happen in the future... the catch, the fish, the sale. False hope will only excite you temporarily if it's not soon replaced with real, solid hope... results!

If it's not, it won't take long for the once fresh excitement to lose its luster because, sooner or later, you'll come to the realization that you can't fillet a nibble and you need more.

So never forget the ultimate goal. We ultimately need to know how many catches got in the boat. It's the difference between someone showing interest and closing the sale. Having someone show interest can be likened to your nibbles. The catches or sales are what you keep. What you keep in the boat is far more important than how many nibbles or calls and leads you have or make. NEVER confuse the two! The moral of the story is don't get overly excited on the nibble, even if you feel like you should. It's the catch that counts. This is the reasoning of a seasoned professional. This will assist in keeping your emotions in check.

It's the catch that counts.

Keeping Your Emotions in Check

If we don't stop the emotional roller coaster between the nibble and the catch we'll end up quitting or, like many who are in sales for years, doing just enough to get by and dragging our feet because we really don't like it. This mindset can be changed. Before I share with you how to change it, let's discuss how it happens.

I've touched on it somewhat already. It starts with the emotional high of the irrational optimism caused by the excitement of the nibble. Then we have the huge emotional let-down when we get a no and the nibble doesn't convert to a catch or a sale.

The next danger is what you say or do immediately after you get your no. What is your attitude and, more importantly, what words come to mind, verbally or non-verbally? It's important to remember that whatever you say next, whether it's negative or positive, creates an association to selling and creates a story.

Let me give you an example. If you made a sale every time you spoke to someone, what thoughts or words would you say to yourself? Let's think of some right now. "Wow, this is incredible. Every time I call someone they say yes and hand me a check. This is so amazing! I must talk to more people. Please, give me the phone. Let me out of the house or the office. I need more leads. Please give me more. My bank account is getting huge." And that's just some of what you might be thinking.

If this were a real world scenario, I'm sure you'd agree that you'd catch on to this great ride after only a few sales. Then after maybe 10 or 20 times, you've bought it, "hook, line, and sinker."

As simple as it sounds what is actually happening is that each time you make a sale you create an incredibly positive association toward calling or contacting people. "Each person I call buys from me! I must keep calling." You'll start thinking this way automatically. Who wouldn't?

What you are actually doing is creating a positive association to making calls because they all turn out so great. You're actually creating a positive story about sales, selling, and your business. You continue to make the story more positive by adding more to it. You could go on and on and on because things are so great.

Now, we know this isn't realistic. But the contrary to it is, unfortunately. You'll get a lot more no's than you will yeses. So instead of creating a positive story or association, we'll lean toward creating a negative one if we're not careful. We do this in the same context as the previous scenario but in a negative way. This is a huge danger for someone new to sales, business, or network marketing. If we're not experienced, a no means that many things can start happening. Let's go over just a few.

You might start to second guess yourself because you can interpret the no as a personal attack or perhaps it hurts your feelings. Maybe you start feeling overly concerned about what others think about you. Note that these thoughts are totally different and opposite than the previous positive ones. If you're not careful your story and negative association toward selling or your products or services gets thicker and thicker, deeper and deeper. "Maybe I'm not cut out for this." But of course if everyone said yes to you these thoughts wouldn't even creep up in your head.

It can really get worse for the new person if they've told anyone about their new adventure of selling. "You're going to do what?" "You don't know a thing about business." "Get a real job," your friends and family spew out at you.

Now those thoughts from your friends and family have a new, stronger familiarity due to recent, painful no's. And your story begins to get worse. But you fight those thoughts off and try again. You get yet another no and another no. The more no's you get, the deeper your plot and story becomes. Each time you attempt and things don't go your way, you attach or stack a deeper plot to your story. The negative self-talk can go out the roof. If you're not careful you may not be able to escape these perceptions, and statistics show that most don't. And this is where failure comes from. It's not from the overwhelming yeses but the overwhelming no's.

To keep from being just another statistic, we have to rewire our story and how we think. This is done by choice, not by chance, and this book is about ways to do this. As I've shared with you earlier, what gives me the ability to keep calling a company over and over for years if need be is that I don't attach a story to the negative results from making all the calls. I'll get into this in greater detail later.

The best way to not create a negative story or association is to not create a negative story or association.

That sounds very simple but it's not as easy as it sounds. When I make a call to someone, I try not to say anything about the call afterwards if my results are not in my favor. If you treat it like nothing, then it will be nothing. If you treat it like the end of the world because they didn't purchase, then it will feel like the end of the world. Who would want to keep going if they feel like it's the end of the world?

I'm not talking about saying positive thinking nonsense like, "I love cold calling, I love cold calling, I love cold calling and everyone is going to like what I have to say." The latter is so not realistic. Look, let me be honest with you. Though I have a reputation of being one of the most persistent, tenacious people you'll ever meet, trust me, cold calling or even just calling isn't my favorite thing and I can't say I love to do it when my attitude isn't right. I'm good at it and certainly don't mind it, but I don't *love* to do it. I feed my attitude by the catch and not the nibble.

Perhaps you've heard the saying, "You must be willing to do the things today others won't do, in order to have the things tomorrow others won't have." I just know if I want to get results it's one of the things that often must be done. It's very possible to master something you don't love to do.

So be very conscious about what you say, especially immediately after what you perceive as negative. It's this personal communication process that gets you programmed deeply with negative junk that makes calling that person back even more challenging. Trust me on this one… it's not the easiest thing when you're behind on your bills, rent, or car payment and life is throwing you a curve ball with personal or family stress. You make a call and someone hangs up on you. This is when you calmly make a note in your file that you called and they hung up and now you calmly but immediately dial another person without hesitation and negative talk about your business or the person that just hung up on you.

When you can master doing this without the negative self-talk, you'll be blown away as to how much more you'll accomplish. The negative self-talk creates a large amount of emotional drag.

Not only are you preventing yourself from developing a negative story, you're also not wasting a lot of energy dwelling on the negative. When you get upset you will find that you waste so much strength and energy to make the next phone call or take the next action step toward your goals that it almost seems next to impossible to move ahead.

We both know that making a call only takes seconds, but when we build up negative emotions and stories, those same calls could take hours to make. And it's this mental fight of thoughts that makes people spend more time thinking about making the next call or taking the next action step than simply *just doing it*. Don't get caught doing the same. It's not what successful people do.

It's hard work to not get overly excited about your nibbles. But try not to. Don't say anything negative about them because they didn't convert and get into the boat with you. And never forget that your ultimate goal is not the nibble but the catch – because you can't fillet a nibble!

Chapter Three
The Three Key Ingredients to Mastering Persistence

Would you be willing to admit that if you were more persistent in certain areas of your life you would get more results in those areas? Sure you would. That's pretty much a given, isn't it?

I want to give you a simple formula that will make you massively persistent toward your goals. I'm a 'tell it like it is' kind of guy, so I'm not going to give you any fluffy stuff here in this book. It's all going to be laser-focused entirely on getting you more results. You'll note that the formula I give you is simple in and of itself, but realistically, mastering it will be the challenge for some. But if you focus on mastering these three things, your income will dramatically increase and you'll attain your goals faster.

I think it's natural for us to make things a bit more complicated in life than they really need to be. We overthink, mentally focus on the 'what ifs,' and otherwise drive ourselves a little nuts. My goal in this book is to give you specific formulas to assist you in becoming more successful. Look at it as a blueprint. Building a house without a blueprint would be a disaster. It would all be a guessing game. Life solutions should not be a guessing game. There is a blueprint for all of our problems and for attaining our goals as well. I will be giving you specific answers or blueprints for mastering the ability to be more persistent in this chapter and throughout this book.

If you know you need to be more persistent and you are not, here is why. First, you are too concerned about what other people think. I don't mean you should be arrogant like, "I don't give a crap what others think about me, I speak the truth." You just let what others think of you roll off of your shoulders. No ego, it just doesn't bother you. Ego sucks out your humility. When you check your ego at the door, you don't even have thoughts of counteracting the person who said something negative about you. It's water off a duck's back. It goes in one ear and out the other.

The second and third reason for not being as persistent as

you'd like to be is that you don't have enough value and belief in yourself or your products or services. It's that plain and simple. Here it is again for emphasis. You're too concerned about what other people think of you, coupled with not having enough value and belief.

Don't make the solution complicated. It truly is this simple. It is now your blueprint to being successfully persistent toward your goals. But just because the answer or solution isn't complicated that still doesn't mean it's always going to be easy to master. If you can focus on mastering these three things, your life will change. This entire book will focus on teaching and helping you master these things.

So allow me to repeat this one more time. It's that important. If you know you need to be more persistent and you are not it's because you are too overly concerned about what other people think about you, coupled with having too low of a value and belief in yourself or your products or services. Let me give you more insight on how all this works.

You're Overly Concerned

Here is how being overly concerned about what other people think prevents you from being massively persistent. Let's see if you can relate to the following: It's time for you to call a potential customer. You make the phone call and they don't answer so you leave a message asking them to call you back.

Several days go by and they don't call you back. You know what your next move should be. It's your job to call them back. And if you're not careful, here is where the self-talk can destroy you. Before even picking up the phone you say to yourself, "I wonder if I'm calling them too early in the morning," or, "I wonder if I'm calling them too late in the day," or, "If they were interested they'd call me back," or, "If I keep calling I might tick them off." I know, you're smiling right now aren't you? We all do this. How much of this negative self-talk you listen to will make or break you.

In this particular example, you can see that the self-talk and negative thoughts exist because you are overly concerned about what other people will think. "What if I wake them up? What if I call too late? What if they get mad at me?" We just "what if" ourselves out of success.

Control Your Own Destiny

Before I go any further let me interject one very important point here. However, you must apply my UCS principle with what I'm about to share. UCS stands for Use Common Sense. Depending on the type of business or sales you're in, *never allow your potential customer to call you*. Again, there are many exceptions to the rule depending on your selling model. So if this doesn't apply... UCS.

In the example above, we called the potential customer and left a message with our number expecting them to call back. Several days passed and we didn't get a call. Problem number one, you've just wasted several days in your selling process because you expected a call back. One that you *knew* you weren't going to receive anyway. What a way to waste your time and now you've gotten further away from the sale.

And here is the second problem with expecting them to call you. It's *your job* to call them, not theirs. If you want to control your own destiny, *you* make the phone call. I may call a customer and just out of courtesy leave a message that includes a call back number, but I know I'm not expecting them to call me back. It's just a normal courtesy to leave the number. If they call me, that's a great bonus. But I NEVER expect it!

When you make the call you're doing the leg work, and that's what you should be doing. You work for a commission or pay. It's your job to work and make the call, not the customer's. I have a strong philosophy when it comes to who calls whom. If I want to do business with you, you can bank on the fact that I'll be calling you. It's how I control my destiny. But if someone wants to do or is doing business with me, they can bank on the fact that I'm *not* calling them. It's their job to call me, not the other way around. It's what they get paid for. If my company starts working with a vendor and they say things like, "We should be done in a few hours, why don't you call me then." That's a good sign that we might not be doing much business with them in the near future unless their thinking changes. They should be calling us.

Never forget that in most cases your customer is a high priority to you but you are not to them. The exception to this – every rule has an exception – is if you're injured and need a doctor. Of course it will be a high priority to you (the "customer" in this case), but the doctor can only focus on one person at a time so if someone else is more severely injured than you are, they will take priority. So include in your mindset that you are going to have to make several attempts.

For example, if I go to drop my car off to have it fixed and the sales person says, "It should be done by noon; call me and I'll let you know." A huge red flag goes off in my head and I start thinking, *Are you kidding? I am your customer and you want me to call you? You must be confused.* I will immediately give them my number and ask them to call me and kindly mention to them that it's their job to make the call, not mine.

If I or my company have people we do business with that expect us continually to call them, we look for someone else to replace them. I take it that seriously and you should, too. So if you're a customer and you allow the people you're doing business with to expect you to call them, it's a sure sign you're not controlling your destiny because you're going to expect your customers to call you as well. If you think this way, stop it now and control your destiny.

If you want to do business with someone, you call them. If they want to do business with you, let them call you.

I hear of people who put out job applications and, because the people they left them with said they'd call them if they were interested, they sit back and complain that they don't have a job or they brag about how many applications they put out. And what happens? Nobody calls them. Take control of your destiny and call, and call, and call again. Go back and drop off the same application. But what if they get upset and say, "I told you that we'd call you if we were interested." Then oh well, don't be overly concerned about what they think and you'll go call the next person you gave an application to that told you the same thing.

Or what if you went back to someone and they said, "Wow, I was just thinking about you! I misplaced your application and I'm so glad you came back!" Or how about this. The person in HR that you gave your application to quit, died, or got fired the very next day. Now the opportunity for you has been totally blown or lost. Lean to this kind of thinking. Throughout this book I'm going to share with you countless success stories on how I took control over my own destiny and you'll see how amazingly things turned out. This is my effort to help you see things differently and encourage you to take a new approach in your own life.

Just to emphasize once more: if you want to do business with someone, you call them. If they want to do business with you, let them call you.

Value and Belief

Now let's complete the final two parts to our formula to being massively persistent. You have to have value and belief. Let me explain. Have you ever wondered why you often know what to do to get results with your goals but you just can't get yourself to do it? For example, people who know they need to lose weight know that if they exercised and burned more calories than they ate or controlled their diet more they'd be successful at losing weight. They know what they need to do but are not doing it.

Another example is creating wealth. Creating wealth starts from saving more than you make. It's not rocket science. But why do so many people live from paycheck to paycheck? They know what they need to do but don't. If you've ever asked yourself the following question, never ask it again.

"How is it that I believe and I know what I need to do but I can't get myself to do it?" The answer is that you don't have a high enough value.

Think of value as the level of importance you place on something.

Again, don't make this complicated. If you believe in your ability to succeed and you believe in your product or services but you don't take action, it's because your level of value is too low. In other words, it's not important enough to you. It really is that simple. If you're not willing to admit this, succeeding will be a far journey for you.

If you look back to the amount of action you've taken toward any goal, it was based on these two things: *value* and *belief*.

You can have all the belief in the world but if you don't place a level of importance on it, you won't take action. The amount of action you take is based upon the amount of value you have. On the flip side, you might have a high value in your product or services and success, but if you don't believe in yourself – once again – you won't take action. You have to master these two things. Let me illustrate this in greater detail.

I'm sure you've been to a personal growth seminar, company rally, or other event before. Often what happens when you leave such an event is that you feel bullet proof, pumped up, and excited – and you can't wait to leave the event, take action, and make things happen. Essentially you're obsessed with taking action. There is a problem with feeling this way, however. Most people, when they leave an event feeling like this, don't know psychologically why they feel this way. And if you can't figure out the why, you certainly can't figure out the how. And the how would be how to feel this feeling and have it keep going consistently for days and even weeks.

So now you leave this event feeling a bit irrationally optimistic. In other words, you're so emotionally high as a kite that you only think about positive results and you irrationally think that everyone is going to say yes to whatever it is you have to offer and wonder why in the world they *wouldn't* listen to you.

Then Monday rolls around and you're doing your thing and you now get a no from a potential customer. Then another no, and another no. Your irrational optimism is starting to bite you in the butt. Then you try to keep going and someone says to you, "Why don't you get a real job!" Family members begin to question your sanity and now that doubt creeps back in.

Before you know it, that feeling of being unstoppable and bullet proof no longer exists. All this can happen to you in an instant. I know you've felt it before. Probably more than you'd like to admit. And again, if you can't figure out why then you can't figure out how to control it. That control would allow you to stop your decline into negative emotions in its tracks and, more importantly, turn it around. If you don't arrest this downward spiral, you're going to crash.

Let me explain to you in detail how this emotional roller coaster begins. When you go to any kind of sales rally or event that's designed to motivate and inspire you, as you're getting dressed to attend, or while driving or flying to the event, or while *at* the actual event, you will either see, feel, hear, or touch something that will immediately change your thoughts.

Do you think these new thoughts are going to be positive or negative? If you said positive you're absolutely right. The atmosphere, music, and all the people together for one common goal is all very exciting. But here is where the first problem begins. Most of the time you are not even consciously aware that you have now created new positive thoughts. The second problem is that we have now allowed these new positive thoughts to instantly change our values and beliefs. That in and of itself isn't the problem. The real problem is that your values and beliefs change instantly and often subconsciously without you even being aware that it's happening.

In other words, you're being totally controlled by external stimuli on both the positive and negative ends of the spectrum. I guess it's okay on the positive side, but if you're not controlling it and you have to wait for something 'good' to happen to make you feel positive, are you really in control? Definitely not! Either way, before you know it you're on an emotional roller coaster. Full of constant ups and downs. Not a fun way to live, wouldn't you agree?

So instead of running away, hiding our feelings, or being a slave to them, doesn't it make more sense to learn how to master those feelings instead? The advantages are endless. How often do you think your values and beliefs can change in a day? They can change tons of times, if you allow it.

If you want to master the ability to control your value and belief system you must first be consciously aware of your thoughts.

Again: If you want to master the ability to control your value and belief system, you must first be consciously aware of your thoughts. Then you must regularly get to a level where you can immediately identify the moment a negative or positive thought creeps up and how it instantly starts changing the way you feel along with how it is affecting your value and belief system.

I'm going to share with you an exercise that I do to constantly strengthen, increase, and test my values and beliefs. Let's say you own some stocks. You'll often hear people tell you not to look at them daily. The reason people say this is because if the stocks go up, then so do your emotions. And if the stocks go down, then so do your emotions. It can make you an emotional basket case. *But only if you allow it.*

Here is how I would put myself through a mental exercise to toughen me up and learn to keep my value and belief system from being so affected by what is going on around me. Before looking at my stock I would prepare myself to mentally see them losing value and also increasing value before getting to the computer screen. I would consciously say to myself, "If I look at them and they're losing value, I'll shrug my shoulders and say, oh well. Perhaps tomorrow will be better." Are you catching on to what I'm actually doing? I'm preparing to ward off any negative thoughts, and more importantly, not allowing them to change my values and beliefs. This is what it takes to be consciously aware of your thoughts.

If I *didn't* do this and prepare my mind, the scenario might go more like this:

Without any mental preparation or awareness, I look at my stocks as they are losing money and instantly I start feeling uncertain and my values and beliefs change immediately. Something I previously shrugged my shoulders at is taken over by uncertainty and it can snowball from there. I get discouraged. I start questioning my decisions. I start questioning my future. And the list could go on and on.

Now keep in mind, all of this happens in an instant and without you even realizing it if you don't plan to ward it off ahead of time.

There are some people who might reason that this is negative. Nonsense! It's realistic.

There is nothing negative about this. It's called preparation. Every time you get in a car and put on a seat belt, whether you realize it or not, you just mentally prepared for a possible accident. You don't usually consciously acknowledge that thought because you've been putting on your seat belt for years. But that is what you are actually doing. Nor did you say to yourself, "It's so negative to prepare for an accident."

If I don't mentally prepare for 'negative' things it could allow a bad situation to get worse. Value and belief could keep crashing. I might now have thoughts that the economy is getting really bad. Then I could go as far as reasoning, "Why bother calling more companies about my services? No one's going to spend money." Thoughts or statements like this are positive proof something as little as checking on your stocks without mentally preparing yourself could totally alter your value and belief system for hours, days, weeks, or longer.

I hope you see how very powerful this is. Mentally toughen yourself up with exercises like this. I'll have more of these exercises for you throughout the book. It's a must-do if you want to master your value and belief system. I call it playing games with your mind instead of your mind playing games with you.

I remember in 2008 sitting in my living room while I was watching CNN as the stocks fell to near what people thought might be depression levels, hitting into the 8,000 mark. I didn't run from it and say, "CNN, that's Constant Negative News." NO! I kept watching and watching. Not only did I keep watch, I recorded it. Then as I kept watching, I could feel my emotions changing. They started becoming negative and creating feelings of uncertainty. So what did I do? I fought it. Not by turning the TV off, though. I kept watching and made more phone calls and took more action toward my goals. This is how you play games with your mind instead of your mind playing games with you. I made more calls, watched the economy crash, and I made even more calls, and more calls after that.

These are the things that I do all day long to mentally keep myself tough and unstoppable. You must do things like this, too. There are people who refuse to watch the news. I can understand that. But I won't refuse to watch it because I allow it to toughen me. How can you expect to be more successful if you don't allow yourself to be mentally toughened and run from what might be painful or negative instead?

Imagine wanting to be in the Special Forces. They don't plan on *only* making you physically tough. You can bet they are going to make you mentally tough as well. They will put you through so many mental exercises that many fail and don't make it. If you agree that it's important for someone in the Special Forces to be mentally tough and you're okay with them having to prove it, then you should be okay with allowing yourself to be mentally tough in life and with your goals… and be willing to prove it.

So how do they prove it? Rest assured it's not by hiding in a cave and quitting. They mentally wear these guys down to see what they can handle. Perhaps no sleep for days. Very little or no food. Someone yelling in their face constantly. Pressing them to the limits physically. All of this is the CNN of the armed forces. It's only negative if you view it that way. Get over it! Is this negative? Yes if you're a wimp, no if you want to be tough! "But Gary, I know I need to be more persistent." Great! Then hang on with me for the ride and don't stop here. Sleep is for sissies! Yes, I'm going to be tough on you, so get ready for mental boot camp!

If you want to be massively persistent and take massive actions toward your goals, allow yourself to be mentally tested. Don't run from it. Run to it, in it, around it, on it, through it, and any other "its" you can come up with. Make up exercises like I did with my stocks. Every time you take action toward a goal or call a customer you can use this as a means to learning how to be more mentally tough, especially when they say no or you can't get ahold of them.

But you're not going to be mentally tough and conditioned if you plan to take action or make calls once a day or once in a blue moon. How ridiculous it would be to think this way. This is serious business. That's like the Special Forces telling you they're only going to feed you twice a day. What's the big challenge in that? How's that going to test you? Tell me I'm not going to eat and sleep for several days and now I'm convinced this is going to be a real challenge.

Keep Mentally Tough and Conditioned

How high is your tolerance to emotional pain? To succeed and keep plowing ahead you must not cower to the slightest problems. Keep pushing yourself purposely to test your limits.

I'll share with you more of some of the things that I do. I certainly don't expect you to push at the level I do but I want to share with you how and what I do to give you an idea of what it means to consciously test and push yourself.

As I'm writing this I've been on the longest, most intense promotional tour ever. I woke up at 4:00am this morning and flew to Phoenix where I spoke at 8:30pm and wrapped up about midnight. Two nights before this I had 4 hours of sleep each night.

This will be my 193rd presentation this year alone. I concluded the year with 202 presentations.

I have mentally pushed myself this year beyond what's normal. Some days I'll have three presentations. I've been in a hotel every day and in different cities for ten months straight. I lug around over 120lbs of luggage. I've had someone rear end me. Left my jacket and bluetooth somewhere on a plane.

Got ready to head to the airport and the car battery was dead. This put me behind to where I nearly missed my flight. I've had my assistant accidently book my flight to the wrong city and we didn't figure it out till I got to the airport. Mistakes are bound to happen when you're keeping a pace like this for nearly a year. Am I wearing you out yet? There's more.

I'll go up to a month without a hug. Months without seeing my friends. I love to cook and don't have that opportunity to get to. I live from hotel to hotel. Each week I have to find my way around a different city. I sleep in different beds with different pillows. My routine has to be recreated every other day or week. I have to get used to a new city constantly. I often forget what day and what city I'm in as they all run together.

After spending the first night in a city I once had to go out to my car and I completely forgot what color the car or make the car was because I rent so many. Recently I attempted to open three cars before I got to what I thought was mine. I'm always hitting the little buttons on the key fob so the lights and horn will go off. I have to get used to driving a different car each day or each week.

I've had four tickets. GPS crashed on me. Just yesterday I took one wrong turn and was lost for an hour. Going through all this takes a certain level of mental toughness. Going through all of this creates an incredible belief and value in what I do because I allow myself to do it. I hope this gives you some insight to what it takes to succeed. You have to test and push yourself.

When I think things are getting very difficult for me I often think of my billionaire hotelier mentor, Gordon 'Butch' Stewart. He owns 23 Sandals and Beaches Resorts. I'm privy to know some of the things that go on behind the scenes of owning such an empire. Trust me when I tell you that this man goes through things on a daily basis that would make the average entrepreneur simply want to throw in the towel and quit.

How does he do it? He's mentally tough. His desire to be mentally tough was driven by his desire to be successful. His values and beliefs are so high he has pushed through the most challenging of times. He simply plows through it. What the average person would view as a huge problem is a cake walk to him.

It's like that Special Forces training. If you can be pushed to go days without sleep and food, then going one day without sleep or food is no longer a challenge. But if you've never pushed yourself to do it, you'll cave. This is the wisdom in looking for ways to get and keep yourself mentally tough. Because when it gets easier, it will be a no-brainer. And then your 'easy' will actually become someone else's breaking point. And eventually an easy day or week to you would make someone else want to quit.

Another mental game I've played in the past is when I feel the emotional weight from getting many no's in a day, I force myself to keep going. My definition of many no's in one day would be from making at the very least 80 to 100 calls and a high percentage of them saying no or not answering. That's a lot to handle in one day.

Now let's imagine we were in phone call boot camp. You're my boot camp sergeant. I feel worn out and get up to sit down in the break room. As my boot camp sergeant, what might you be saying? "Coxe, get up off your butt and get back on those phones NOW! Move it. No time for sissies. You say you want results, well you're not going to get them sitting here like a loser. Got that? Now get up and start dialing!"

This is the actual type of dialog I would give myself. I still use this self-talk. Because this is what will toughen you mentally. You must listen to your drill sergeant. Don't just hear and say the self-talk. Actions speak louder than words. So get up and take action... NOW!

Get out there in the mental trenches and test and push *yourself*.

Can't you see this type of attitude in phone call boot camp? It would be no different from basic training. It's designed to toughen and strengthen you. You're pushed to the limits to see what you are capable of doing. I personally would test myself to see how many calls I could make in one day and what kind of results I would get from that effort. One day I remember doing 137 dials. How can you not get results doing that much? If you remove the emotional self-talk that attacks us it removes all of your emotional drag, leaving you with more energy to move ahead faster.

Stay mentally tough with exercises like this that will push and test your values and beliefs to the limit. Don't wait to be forced to have them tested this way. Get out there in the mental trenches and test and push *yourself*. Don't be overly concerned about what others think and master the ability to play games with your mind instead of your mind playing games with you as you keep your values and beliefs high and strong.

Chapter Four
The Real Difference Between
Being Passive or Persistent

You have two choices when it comes to taking action toward your goals. You can do it passively or you can be persistent. Let's take some time and determine what the side effects are between the two.

Often when we think of the words 'side effects' we associate something negative with it. It's like those crazy commercials on TV that advertise anti-depressant medication and then they tell you all the side effects. Anti-depressant pills that can cause suicidal thoughts. Wow! Really?

Let's go over the side effect of being passive first. When I teach a seminar, I ask the audience to write down the word passive. Then to the right of that I have them put down the side effect. So here it is. The side effect of being passive is, "I will be poorer!" Yes, I use the word 'poorer' instead of 'poor' for a reason. Someone who makes $50,000 is *poorer* than someone who makes $100,000. Someone who makes $100,000 is *poorer* than someone who makes $200,000, and so on. Now that you know the side effects of being passive, just fill in the blanks below for emphasis.

Passive: "I _____ be _____."

It's time to discuss the side effects of being persistent. Be careful not to get too far ahead of yourself by blurting out the answer as you might not get it correct. People will often say out loud that the side effect of being persistent is being 'richer,' but that's the farthest from the truth. Being richer is a positive byproduct of being persistent and by no means a negative side effect. The negative side effect of being persistent is the following: "I will tick people off!"

Don't make this complicated. You'll either be passive and be poorer or persistent, know that you'll tick some people off, but you'll be richer and more prosperous. And now that you know the side effect of being persistent, just fill in the blanks below for emphasis once again.

Persistent: "I will _____ people _____!"

You can be the most passive person in the world and only talk to ten people in a year. A percentage of people are simply just not going to like you. They may not like you because of what you are selling, your skin color, your perfume or cologne, your looks, your clothes, your attitude, or whatever else. Perhaps they woke up on the wrong side of the bed. You just don't know.

They brought Jesus Christ up on trump charges and killed him. Not everyone is going to like you. It only makes sense to play bigger numbers then, knowing the same percentage of people are not going to like you. But you're going to get a lot more results.

It's obvious that this should make all the sense in the world, but why is it often so hard to follow through on this concept? Knowing and doing are two totally different things as I'm sure you would agree. Much of the answer is what we have discussed in the previous chapter. If we have a low belief and value in ourselves and our products or services we will be overly concerned about what other people think about us. We have to learn to master this concept.

A simple way to illustrate this is through a question: Would you feel a little uncomfortable going to three of your neighbors' houses at 2:00am and banging on their doors as loud as you can? You certainly would, especially if there was no reason for doing this.

Now let's look at it another way. Would you feel a little uncomfortable going to three of your neighbors' houses at 2:00am and banging on their doors if their homes were on fire? You certainly wouldn't! Same action, knocking loudly on the doors, but a different response and purpose. It's changed this time because you believe you're offering a service – knocking on the door to save lives – that helps someone. You value your fellow neighbors' lives.

You may not even like them, but you go knocking. Would you care if they yelled at you immediately after you knock? Absolutely not. You're on a mission to save lives and you're not going to stop until you can do whatever it takes to get the attention of someone in the house.

You have to learn to have a similar fever, passion, value, and belief in your life as well. When your value and belief are high you just keep going through all the obstacles. Nothing will stop you. Let me share with you an example of what it means to jump through hoop after hoop to get results as a means of illustrating this point for you.

I know of a case where a lady who was going through a difficult time in her life and reached out in a negative way to criticize someone who we'll call Jay. The lady didn't personally know Jay. She criticized him and wrote that he didn't care at all about people. Jay decided to do a little research and find out more about that person by checking her page. While taking a little time, he saw something on this lady's social media page that seemed disturbing.

She wrote to everyone, "I will be leaving you... all the best!" Jay read that and took it seriously. He didn't hang around passively. He took immediate action to help out. He noticed that all the comments under this lady's statement went something like this: "I'm praying for you," or, "If you need anything my number is...." Seriously? If someone is threatening suicide, telling them you're praying for them and offering your phone number isn't what's needed. Unfortunately, people do and say things like this truly meaning well but it is certainly not effective.

Jay persisted and did some detective work. He noticed on her page what city she lived in and tried to also strike up a conversation with her through email. She responded in desperation.

While emailing back and forth with this lady he saw someone who had written something that seemed to have known her who posted their number. Jay called it. He wasn't going to give up. It turned out that this person had only met her once. Jay refused to stop there and asked this lady if she knew anyone who knew her. The lady by chance had the phone number of the brother of this desperate woman.

Jay called him and got voicemail. He called again and again. The lady's brother finally picked up but was out of town, but Jay explained what was going on. Jay emailed this woman his number hoping she would call as he waited for a reply. The next thing he did as he was writing her was to call what he thought was the local police department in her town.

After the first call to the police department Jay was given yet another number for another district closer to her location. He still persisted and called that next number as well. As he was doing this he was also sending her emails to create more dialog with her. The police officer on the other end said that he had known of the name of the person but didn't know where she lived. Jay asked if they could stop by and check on her. Jay also explained the situation and said that while he was talking to the officer he was writing her. The officer asked Jay if he could ask her for her address. Jay in turn asked the officer to look it up because he didn't want to take the chance of stopping the dialog by asking her a question like that. He wanted to make sure the communication didn't stop until someone got to her home.

Her emails were getting more desperate and it seemed apparent that she might commit suicide. Jay asked the officer if he would supply his cell number so that if she offered her address he could text it to the officer immediately. The officer refused but Jay replied, "I can't take the chance of having her call me and then hang up on her to call you back to give you her address if I get it. It's too great of a risk. This way if I get her on a call I can keep talking to her while texting you her address if she chooses to share it."

The officer refused to give his cell number out. Jay respectfully responded, "You have a possible suicide case here and you are refusing to give out a cell number to perhaps save a life." He continued, "Imagine what that's going to look like to the media and public if she does commit suicide." He still refused.

Are you seeing the 'never give up' attitude and persistence? It's ruthless and never-ending. As all this was going on, people were still posting messages like, "If you need me call me!" Jay called the police back to let them know he hadn't made any progress getting any more information from her other than maintaining a dialog. The officer said that they were finally able to find her house and that they now had the situation under control. Jay received an email from this lady the following day saying, "Thank you!"

Imagine if you jumped through hoops toward your goals this passionately and consistently. You would never hesitate when there is an obstacle. Jay went above them, through them, around them, and over them, and even reprimanded an officer to get results. He would not accept a no. If you looked at all your goals in such a manner you'd come up with some of the most impossible ways to make things happen. Be that committed.

Be that committed.

Is there a goal you've been wanting to make a reality but you just haven't been this committed? Jay was committed to making sure this lady was going to get help. He never gave up. Nothing got in his way. If you have this much passion, determination, and focus you'll reap the results. Oh, it may not be in a few days, months, or even years, but properly directed action that is compounded will eventually get results.

Playing Chess with the TSA Landed Me in Jail?

Here is one final story for you before we wrap up. Now who would dare play games with the Transportation Security Administration (TSA)? Oops... yours truly. I was on a recent flight from Charlotte to Florida for presentations in Tampa and Miami. When I'm not using my own aircraft to get around, I go commercially, and oh how I dislike going through TSA security!

You know the drill... take off your jacket, remove shoes, and take out all your liquids. Now, there are times I travel five or more times in one week. That's a lot of, "Take off your jacket, remove shoes, and take out all your other stuff."

So, I decided to try a little experiment. Could I save myself some time and frustration if I didn't have to unzip all my bags and pull everything out? I usually carry lots of cable, electronics, and cameras as well. Keep in mind, they usually don't like to have you keep that stuff in your bags. If I don't pull them out and they find them, I have to wait even longer to have TSA re-inspect and nose through my bags again.

Would it be worth leaving all this stuff in my bag? And no, if I'm 'caught' I won't go to jail... they will just ask to inspect my baggage and eat up more of my time. I do, however, before letting the bag through, mention to the inspector who monitors the screen as the bags are run through that I have lots of wires and electronics.

And the experiment begins. Do you know for every 20 or so times I go through TSA I might get stopped once? Isn't that interesting? One out of 20. Now please don't get me wrong. I'm by no means encouraging people to ignore rules and policies, or other authority figures for that matter! However, it's interesting how programmable we are and how willing we are to follow someone else's path when at times the path may not even make sense.

I saved myself tons of time and, more importantly, lots of aggravation by not pulling out all my equipment. The only way I knew if my little experiment would fail or not is to create a track record and try... Let's say on my first time through TSA I get 'busted.' Now what... quit? I didn't have enough of a track record to make an intelligent decision yet. So I didn't give up.

Sometimes you can't – or won't – find the answers to things unless you try and beta test or create a track record for days, weeks, months, or even longer. This is important because if we always base our opinions on one or two experiences we're going to take the 'assume' role all the time. We'll often assume that's just the way it is and that it's always been done that way, whether it's true or not. You know what they say about those who assume. It's always better to form opinions in an educated and informed manner.

Chapter Five
Are You Smart or Stupid? Marketing 101

So... do you want to be smart in your business or stupid? Of course we all want to be smart. In this chapter you will soon see that if we don't learn to play games with our minds instead of our minds playing games with us, we can become very stupid very quickly and hurt our own sales and income.

Being successfully persistent can often boil down to how good you are in your own personal marketing. Let me explain why and what I mean when I say this. It's a given that in marketing you usually have two ways of pursuing leads. These numbers are only examples in principle.

You can call one thousand customers once (1000 x 1) or you can call one hundred customers ten times (100 x 10). The concept behind these numbers is that you must regularly keep yourself in front of your potential customers. Once is not enough. I call it 'dripping' on them.

If you send out direct mail pieces it's far more effective to mail out 100 cards 10 times instead of 1,000 cards once.

So then, 100 x 10 is SMART!
And   1000 x 1 is STUPID!

Which one do you want to be? I'll base my next argument here strictly on making phone calls or being in front of a potential customer. Too often I'll observe people that call leads only once and, if the potential customer doesn't call back, they toss the lead. Or if they say no it gets tossed as well.

Doing this is as good as taking your cash and lighting it on fire. What a waste of money! Never forget that *all* leads cost you. Whether you literally paid for it or it cost you in time (to get the lead, write it down, ask for it, or the time it took you to think about calling or making the call), all leads cost you money.

All leads cost you money.

Here are some statistics I recently read that I think you might find interesting. See where you fit.

48% of sales people never follow up with a prospect.
25% of sales people make a second contact and stop.
Only 10% of sales people make more than three contacts.

2% of sales are made on the first contact.
3% of sales are made on the second contact.
5% of sales are made on the third contact.
10% of sales are made on the fourth contact.
80% of sales are made on the fifth to twelfth contact.

After reading those stats it certainly doesn't take a rocket scientist to figure out which one of these are smart and which are stupid. I believe that most people don't hit the 80% mark on the list because they are too overly concerned about what other people think and their value and belief about themselves and their products and services are way too low.

Leads are too valuable to simply discard or toss away. I remember once going into an office that had a sales team. In this particular case there was a lady in charge of training a few people on how to follow up on leads. All the leads were written down on a piece of paper. The paper was made up of rows and columns. It was filled with names and numbers from top to bottom. With a small team at her side listening in, she started making calls. One after another. Each person that said no, she crossed a line through their name and went on to the next one.

The first problem I saw was that she had all of her leads on a piece of paper.

If you have all your leads on a piece of paper you don't have enough leads.

You want to have so many leads that it's virtually impossible to remember all of the conversations you've had with each one. And if you have a really good memory then you should have so many leads that you forget where you were in conversation last with a lead.

I kept leads on a piece of paper *decades* ago. If you're serious about sales and serious about following through, you must have some kind of database to organize and track your process, sales, last conversation, next conversation, and so on. So don't forget that if you have your leads on a piece of paper you don't have enough leads.

The second issue I saw while observing this woman is that after a no she just crossed their names out and moved on to the next one. If you go back to those stats that I shared with you, that puts her up on the top of the list. And that's a list no one should want to be on top of: the 48% of sales people who never follow up with a prospect.

What do you want to bet if this lady was caught complaining about her lack of sales that she just might want to blame it on things like, "no one seems interested," "it's such a bad economy," "these leads are no good," or any other excuse that we all have a tendency to make. I think this makes for an interesting observation. So before making excuses as to why our sales aren't where we'd like them to be, let's point the fingers at ourselves first. I think you'll find in most cases that's where the answer *really* lies.

Being that this lady had all of her leads on a few sheets of paper, it would have been impossible to organize a system to follow up effectively. If you have a lead that you think is a candidate for your product or services and they have told you no, by no means dismiss that number. We need to call back or perhaps send an email, sample of our product, or a postcard. You'll have to determine when. It may be the next day, next week, next month, or next year. Follow up. Place the lead in a database and tag or task it to remind you in the future to try again.

I hope I've made a very convincing argument that calling 100 people 10 times makes a lot of sense. The challenge is doing what we know we need to be doing. If we know this will make a difference in our sales then why is it so hard to make several or more calls to the same people? Let's continue to discuss this further.

Watch Your Story

One reason why it's so very difficult to keep calling people back or contacting them through other means is because they have said no or don't call back and we subconsciously create little stories in our minds that we also – unfortunately – listen to.

I shared this with you in the previous chapter, how we start putting things in our minds when the potential customer doesn't call back. We go into excuse mode without even realizing it. "Maybe I'm calling them too early in the day. They might think I'm pestering them. Maybe I'm calling them too late."

I want you to be aware that you do this *all the time*. You have to stop listening to these stories. Perhaps there is a better way to explain this… you have to stop *obeying* these stories. They will always be there and you will always hear or listen to them but you must not obey them. I think you'd be shocked how many times you obey your own stories that don't benefit your life even outside of your career. You create them on every subject from health, relationships, spirituality, finances, and much more. We all do this. But some do it many times more than others.

Here is an additional mindset I want you to adopt. If a name pops up on your database to be called, then call it immediately. It doesn't take all day long to call 20 or 30 people unless you're reading each one a book. What keeps people from making lots of calls in a short time is the story and negative self-talk they allow between calls.

Some companies have what's called a predicated dialer. What this means is that when a person hangs up the phone the predicated dialer immediately calls the next person. It doesn't have a mind of its own. It doesn't say to itself things like, "I wonder if I'm calling too early, I wonder if I'm going to tick them off if I call again, I wonder if I'm going to be calling them too late in the day. Last time we spoke they didn't seem that interested, why bother calling again."

It just calls and calls and calls. Become like that predicated dialer. Don't think about what story you have attached to that name and number, just call. Create your own personal phone call boot camp and get immersed in it. You might have to start by making your boot camp last only 30 minutes, then an hour, then two. I've toughened myself up to where I can go for 10 hours if need be.

If you have a group of people on a team or you're a manager, allow your team to give you permission to 'get in their faces' so to speak and try this out. You'll be amazingly surprised what kind of results you'll see.

What makes this even more challenging is that when you attempt to make that second, third, fourth, or even fifth call or contact, you keep stacking more junk onto your story with each contact. Your plot gets bigger and bigger. It's as if you subconsciously start to justify and validate why you *shouldn't* keep calling. You reason, "I've called several times now. It's obvious they aren't interested. If they were they'd pick up the call or at the very least call me back."

But let's look at the reverse of this reasoning. We see how we have a hard time making calls when we get no responses or get a no. If we were to get a yes on every call would we tend to make more calls? Of course we would. We still create a story but the story is a lot different. This time is goes like this. "Every time I make a call someone picks right up away and they purchase my product. I call them back again and they buy something else. It never fails!" This is a story too, and because you obey the story, it makes it easy to keep calling in this case. But unfortunately this isn't the real world and that's why so many fail to succeed. It is, however, an example of how we create a story. We create both positive and negative stories.

How aware are you on every call you make that before, after, and even during your call you are creating a story? The first step to not obeying it is being aware that it's talking to you. If you can't get to that point regularly you will obey it every time. The story becomes so real to you that you can't see any way *not* to obey it. In your mind's eye, it seems so real. It seems this way because we all have a tendency to take the course of least resistance along with looking for excuses. This gives us a way to make excuses and escape, but it won't get us results.

Disobeying Your Negative Story… Master This and You WIN!

Let me share with you the value of learning to master your ability to *not* obey your story. This is an example that made me thousands of dollars. I had received a lead from a gentleman who appreciated my work and materials. The lead he gave me was his regional manager. I called and called over several months with no return phone call. I finally got him and he told me that he really wasn't the right contact. I wish I would have known that months before. He finally gave me his manager's information.

I started the process all over again. I finally got through. His name was Lee. I gave Lee our 'pitch' and he seemed somewhat interested but certainly not overly excited. Being in a state of total awareness got me to think, "Okay, Gary, be careful not to read into the fact that he didn't seem too interested. Maybe he's had a bad day."

So a few days later it was time to call back and the self-talk began. I specifically remember him not appearing to be that interested but I disobeyed the thought that immediately came to my mind when his name came up for me to call him. It was, "Why bother." I disobeyed and called again… and again.

I finally got through and he told me that he didn't think he had a slot for me to speak but if I called back in a week he'd have an answer. I called back in a week and got no answer. I called and called again. Still no answer. What could the story now include? "Well, Gary, it's obvious that he is not interested. He specifically told you to call him back and now you're calling and he's totally ignoring you. If he was really interested he'd at least call you back."

A week or so later it was time to call him again. How did I know it was time? Not because it's on a piece of paper, but because I have a database that reminds me to call him and I hope you have this, too. Before I called him I looked over the previous notes. I did notice something that instantly added to my negative plot of a story. We had Lee's email and he was regularly receiving emails from me. On the software we use we can tell if a person chooses to opt out or no longer cares to hear from us by not getting our emails any longer. It's marked with a red X.

Imagine the story now. "Gary, you've been trying to do something with this company for many months. The guy certainly doesn't seem that interested. He never takes your call. When he does pick up he tells you to call back again. You have to call and call and call even when he tells you to call back. On the last call he told you that it doesn't look good that they even have time to fit you in to speak. And now you've got that red X so it's very obvious to you that he has opted out of your emails and doesn't want to have any of your information. Why would you waste time calling?"

I know you've done this before as well. All my self-talk, though, isn't totally based on concrete facts, is it? Some of this story might be an assumption. I really don't know. If I obey the story, I will end up sitting on the sidelines and I will have a 100% chance of losing. But if I disobey the story and get in the game I have at least a 50/50 chance of winning and those odds are better than the ones on the sidelines or in the bleachers.

So I disobeyed my story, even though it was yelling at me loud and clear, "You're probably wasting your time. He's opted out. He doesn't even want to receive your emails anymore."

Lee finally picked up and agreed to bring me in to present to his team.

A few months later I showed up to speak to his management team of about 30 people. In my presentation I got into the subject of persistence and shared with everyone my story about following through with Lee. I then told everyone that we could tell that Lee opted out his email which caused me to think that he really wasn't interested.

Being that the group was small, Lee kindly interrupted me and said, "I didn't opt out of your emails."

"What are you talking about?" I responded. "Are you sure? I get an indication when someone does with a red X on their file and got one on yours."

He said, "That wasn't me. It must have been our server as it obviously didn't recognize your email."

Wow! I was doing back flips in my mind. What a victory in not listening to my story and blatantly disobeying it. All this time I thought that he opted out and really wasn't interested. I'll never believe that little red X again! It got better. At the end of my presentation he announced to all of his managers that he would allow them to expense any of my programs they wanted to purchase and he would pick up the tab to have me speak in their regions. Now that's a huge success story because I disobeyed my self-talk.

And by the way, I can tell you success story after success story like this. How is it that I can do this? Because I consciously make it a point to remember them. It validates why I should disobey my negative self-talk. I have valid proof. I keep track of these results and never forget them.

The only reason I have so many of these stories is because I have made thousands and thousands of calls. I made so many calls in my early years that I would use the telephone so much on my left ear that it is closer to my head than my right ear. I'm not exaggerating. It's not a birth defect. That's what happens when you make one to two hundred phone calls a day for years.

My point in telling you this is when you buy into what I'm telling you and you keep making call after call you will have so many success stories because of disobeying your own negative thoughts that you'll have no desire to make excuses. You'll have validation after validation that what you're doing works and it's the right way to get results.

People who don't think this way have the wrong attitude and validate why they should listen to their negative story. This causes them to cave in which causes them to delete that lead and go on to the next. And remember, we shared together earlier that this process was what? Yes, it was stupid. Let's not be stupid at this so we can get more results.

It's Just Alphabet Soup

I often will jump through as many hoops as I can to get through to a potential customer. One option is texting. Before I share this next example with you it must be said that when you call or contact a business as opposed to consumers you can usually make more calls regularly to contact them. They may have a receptionist to take calls. They might have a direct work number and a cell number. How and when (and how often) you contact them will depend on the situation. This is where you must UCS: Use Common Sense.

There was a company that I did a lot of work for out in the sales field. They had offices throughout the country and I did presentations at many of them. I was also able to collect a lot of testimonials while at those offices. This often gives me more credibility and dramatically increases my value, so much so that I'll be even more persistent because once they see the testimonials, their value will also increase.

Remember, cost is only a concern in the absence of value.

So I had lots of strong testimonials to back my work up. There was one business owner that I tried over and over to contact who was a part of this company. During a period of time I texted his assistant over twenty times and this gentleman another 23 times... and yes, I counted.

He finally picked up when I attempted to call. Sure he was a bit bothered by my continuing to try to contact him. He said, "Why do you keep texting and calling?" I respectfully replied, "I don't attach a story to your name and number when I call you. It's just a name with a number. Every time I call you it's like starting from scratch. Imagine, if half of your sales team had that mindset how much would their sales increase?"

And he invited me in to speak to his team and was very pleased. Now seriously, how much time does it physically take to make the actual call or text a message... seconds. So to make 15 to 20 calls, plus talk time could be done in an hour depending on your script. But why can so many people barely make 15 or 20 calls in a day, or a week for that matter? It's because they create, script, and obey their negative stories between calls, texts, and emails. They mentally battle back and forth and back and forth, waste precious time, and use their story to justify why they should put off calling. And this is why so many people in sales are not productive. It's all because of a head game they haven't learned to win.

When you see a number on your computer screen that you need to call or on your phone that you need to text, remember that the names and numbers you see are just parts of the alphabet. It's all alphabet soup. There are a bunch of numbers and letters from your alphabet soup that happen to make up the names and phone numbers of people you need to call. If you make it more than just alphabet soup you'll be creating negative associations that will slow you down and make you poorer.

Watch Out for Double Jeopardy – This is Very Dangerous

It's extremely important to make sure common sense dictates to us that if you are this consistent and persistent, sooner or later someone is going to pick up the phone and be upset with you. Duh! Don't forget the other alternative. Passive is poorer. There is no way around this.

If you DO NOT have a defense for what and why you're doing what you're doing, trust me on this... you'll be shot down so fast you won't know what hit you. Not to mention you'll question every empowering belief you've been creating that is associated with being persistent. And now, instead of validating why you should never give up, you will now justify why you *should* give up, slow down, or stop.

Here is a powerful case in point. But before I get to it let me first make a very important argument in regards to calling someone who replies and is rude to you for trying to contact them. Never forget that you can call a person only once or twice and that call could set them off. You can't read people's minds. You just never know what will happen.

Then again, I've called people 20 times before they picked up and when they did they were excited that I kept calling because they had lost my number, their phone fell in the toilet, or someone stole it and they lost all their numbers. Never forget to think this way. If you're going to continue to be successful you must err on the persistent side, not the passive.

Haven't you tried calling a friend before many times and something like this happened? You could justify calling them many times because you're friends. So you call and call and call to finally have them answer and tell you that their phone was stolen, lost, or just quit working.

Here is my answer to figuring out how many times you should attempt to contact someone. You're not going to like this answer. Here it is: I don't know the answer. Do you know why I don't know the answer? It's because I don't have a crystal ball. I can't predict the future. In other words, I have no idea what the person that I'm about to call is going to be thinking, whether they will answer after one ring or five, or whether they will pick up the first call or the 19th.

If I could see through a crystal ball I might be able to see that right before I'm about to make a phone call, the person I'm trying to contact just had an argument with their spouse. It might not be a good time to call now. So I do and they're agitated and take it out on me and hang up. If I were to call again at another time they'd be much more receptive. You just don't know and can't predict this.

But the best way I can answer this is to help you understand that you will always try to take the course of least resistance. This is human nature. So whether you should call twice, ten times, each day, or each month or year. This should be considered even more if you are thinking about ways *not* to follow through, and the REAL reason is because you're overly concerned with what they might think coupled with having too low of a value and belief system. Ask yourself that question before each call that you don't want to make; that should give you your answer.

Let me warn you about double jeopardy. This is where you have a limited belief or story attached to a person's name like the example I shared with you earlier with Lee. I'll explain further with this next example. I was in California some time ago filming a TV show. I was there for over a week. I figured while I was there that I would contact a local company and offer my services to them while I was in town. I had done work for hundreds of his colleagues in other parts of the United States already.

I called the manager about three times and left one message. I then stopped in unannounced to see if he would give me just two minutes of his time. He refused. Then I noticed that his business card was on the front receptionist's desk and included his cell number. You know I snagged that card! So I called that a few times. Then he finally picked up. He wasn't the happiest camper.

He said, "I noticed you called several times. Don't you think if I was interested I would have called you back?" This could very well be a valid point.

It is at this very moment that you must master what you say, and more importantly, your thoughts; here is why. If you don't, you can allow what he just said to you to completely destroy your belief and your mindset that allows you to keep pushing ahead and not give up.

Think for a moment about what he said. "Don't you think if I was interested I would have called you back?" It certainly seems to be a valid argument. But you must not believe that it's totally true.

You have to immediately counteract such a thought.

The reason you must do this is that your mind will try to tell you all day long that what he said is right. Oh yes, there is some truth to his comment but if you don't know how to properly counteract this verbally with him and in your own mind, you're going to mentally be up a certain creek without a paddle.

If you allow his comment to validate his belief that if he was interested he would have called you, what do you think is going to happen to you once you make another call and someone doesn't answer and you get ready to try again? It can be very dangerous.

You'll reason like this. "I've already tried to contact this person once. If they were truly interested they would call me back, right?" You now question yourself. You have now bought into the negative self-talk and you will immediately become passive. If you keep repeating what he said to yourself and replaying that recording in your mind you will be limiting yourself to one call per potential customer if you are not careful. And don't forget, we know that this is what...? Stupid! Let's not be stupid about our success.

I'll tell you in a moment how I handled this but first, when something like this happens, whether you feel you've handled it successfully or not, you better get back on the phone *immediately* and start another call. Doing this helps you instantly start counteracting any possibility toward buying into the belief that people will call you back if they're truly interested.

Now here is where it can get worse and knock you out for the count. If you don't regularly make lots of calls or attempts to contact customers, the longer you wait to make the next call, the more time you have to build up the story to validate that you shouldn't call someone more than once because they'd call you back if they were interested. The more time you wait between calls, the more time you have to crush your own mental strength and persistence. You must refuse to allow this to happen. By refusing to allow this to happen and immediately moving ahead, you truly play games with you mind instead of your mind playing games with you. When I say immediately, I mean *immediately* make the next call. Don't wait one minute or five minutes or a few days. Get on the next call ASAP and this will help knock out any possible validation from the comments of the last person you spoke to. I can't emphasize this enough. You're going to be up a creek if you hardly have any leads and a call like this happens when you don't have any more leads to call immediately.

So here was my respectful response to this man. "Sir, I'm sorry to have made you feel bothered." (Don't ignore his feelings, respect them.) With a respectful chuckle I continued, "I never know when calling someone back and they don't call me back if they didn't lose their phone, it fell in the toilet, or if they even got my message. I'd rather be a bit more persistent than passive." It didn't go over well in this particular case, and needless to say, I didn't get in.

If you're going to choose to be persistent and not passive, you will tick some people off. There is no way around this. It's like Babe Ruth having no choice but to strike out so much because he's up to bat so often. You can't get around this.

But you MUST role play and make sure you have a respectful comeback when someone questions why you're so persistent. Here are some examples.

"I didn't mean to upset you. But I can assure you that, if you're looking for someone to sell your house, you want someone who believes in what they do enough to avoid being passive and sitting by, *hoping* they'll sell your house. Hope alone doesn't sell houses. You want someone who is going to work hard for you. You can be assured I *will* work hard for you because I get results."

Here is one I sometimes use when trying to contact an organization that has a sales team: "I didn't mean to upset you. As you might know, the average sales person stops at one attempt. They say the above average sales person stops at three. I teach people to become well above average and that gets everyone more results. Wouldn't you like to see more results from your sales team?"

Don't stop here. You must create your own comebacks, because if you don't, the double jeopardy will win every time and you'll begin to believe it. Having a comeback is how you mentally fight your negative beliefs. Without them, you'll be passive with less results.

This Might be an Epiphany for You

Keep in mind if you're not used to having comebacks like this in your regular dialog when contacting customers, I can assure you that you're way more passive than persistent! If you lean more toward being persistent, you will have to prepare strong comebacks. If you can't fire off the tip of your tongue what I just shared with you or something similar, you're either not persistent enough or you're not getting in front of enough people.

Even if you're passive and get in front of a lot of people, someone is still bound to be unhappy with you trying to contact them. If you're not prepared with a comeback, you'll hesitate on being persistent because you'll be at a loss for what to say, which will make you feel stupid or ineffective. So, in an effort not to feel that way, you won't prepare a comeback and you certainly won't allow yourself to be persistent enough to put yourself in a position of needing a comeback.

You Must Create Your Own Respectful Comebacks

This will be your missing link in being massively persistent. I remember the first time I used the one I just shared with you about, "The average person stops at one...." I was actually face to face with someone. My comeback sounded like this was the first call I ever made in my life. It was awful. I stammered and stuttered through the whole thing. Why? It was new to me. I hadn't wired myself with enough comebacks. It toughened me, though. I did a bad job only because it was the first time I said it face to face. The second time will get better, the third better than that, and so on. You might remember stammering and stuttering on your sales calls when you first started. But you got over it. View this the exact same way.

Here is another example. I called this particular gentleman for four years. That's right, four years. Each and every time he took my call, which wasn't often, he kindly said no and that he wasn't interested. And in the same kind manner I said, "Thank you and thanks also for taking my call when you didn't have to." A response like this is very important. Go overboard to be kind, whether they are or not. If you feel you have to fake it to be kind then that's okay because it tells you that you perhaps really aren't that way in these kind of situations and now you must learn the difference between being kind and becoming kind. If you make enough calls like this, you'll learn it's easier to become kind instead of forcing it. This takes time, but when you master becoming kind, no one will get under your skin. Becoming kind removes the friction when it comes to making the next call if the last person was rude or you didn't get the results you were expecting.

After four years he took another call and finally said yes. He brought me in several times to speak to his organization. I will always remember the kind words he said about me before introducing me on stage in front of about 500 people.

Becoming kind removes the friction when it comes to making the next call if the last person was rude or you didn't get the results you were expecting.

He shared with everyone that I had been calling him for four years. He began to relate to them that after four years he started to become more and more intrigued. "What is it that this man has that he can keep calling me for four years and every time I tell him no he is so kind about it and then calls back three or four months later to see if I have changed my mind?"

The information that I'm sharing with you is the same information in a nutshell that I was able to share with his organization. He told me many months later that his sales have consistently increased and he knows for a fact that it's because of the program that he allowed me to share. I'm happy to say I have his endorsement for life.

I hope this makes some very strong points for you and illustrates why it's so important to be persistent, and the many advantages of doing so.

How Not to Attach a Story

It's important to know that there are ways to help you counteract attaching a negative story to your leads. The novice might find it hard to master what I'm about to share with you due to their inexperience. But mastering this will make the cold-calling process easier.

Never forget that what you say verbally or non-verbally immediately after a call will be subconsciously remembered and added to the script in your story. This makes things worse for you. When you say things like, "What a liar!" "Buyers or liars!" "Just another tire kicker wasting my time!" and statements like this, you are just adding more barnacles onto the side of your ship. Do you think barnacles on the hull of a ship speed it up or slow it down? You know the answer to that. Always remember that each time you trash-talk someone, you are adding more and more barnacles to that potential customer's story.

Now imagine making 20, 50, or 80 calls a day and after each call you add more barnacles. And then you keep doing this for days or weeks. You can easily see why making calls or following up can be so difficult. Clean the barnacles off. And even better, don't let them hang on for the ride. How do you do that? After the call, simply zip up your mind and go on to the next. Zipping up keeps the barnacles off the ship.

Keep in mind that people don't call you back or take your calls for many reasons. Often it's that the timing may not be right. But when it is, if your competition is in front of them instead of you, take a guess who loses the game?

Here are just a few reasons why people say no or just don't

take your call and respond. They may be having a bad day. Haven't you ignored a call because you were having a bad day?

Haven't you shown interest in a product before and then, when the sales person called you back, you shot them down or didn't take their call because you were in a bad mood or the timing was bad, even if you were still interested?

Here's a perfect example of that. Just yesterday I was in a store, waiting in line to buy something. The store was very loud. A gentleman called me whom I had spoken to before. He told me a week before that he'd call me back the very next day with an answer to my question. If I purchased his product it would have been a $12,000 sale. First, I was aggravated that he called me four days later. And remember, because he's trying to make a sale with me I am not going to call him back to find out what's going on. That's not my job. What I actually did was call his competition, who charges $16,000 for the same service.

When he called me back, I was a little frustrated because I was expecting someone else's call and mistook the number for his. Plus I lost my place in line because I had to run out of the store where it was quieter to take the call. I finally realized who it was. I told him that he was supposed to call me days ago and I've gone to his competition to check them out and it looks like I'm going there. It had to be very obvious to him that I was rushed and aggravated because it was so loud in the store, and then I had to run out and take the call on top of the fact that he was supposed to call me days ago. What it boils down to is that he blew it.

Now if I was him I would have read into the fact that I was aggravated and, more importantly, *why* I was. I gave him all the clues on the call. Then if I were him I would have called back in a day or two and apologized. "Gary, I'm sorry to have called you while you were in line at the store. (He obviously would have known I was in line because I told him.) I know I should have called you when I told you I was going to. I do, however, have the answer to your question. If you're okay with it, can I still share it with you or call you back in an hour or so?" I was still in a frame of mind that I could be won over, especially if I was going to save over $4,000. I would have had so much more respect for him. But it never happened.

Maybe the next person you call, like me, was totally distracted. The timing could be wrong, they are in a bad mood, having problems at home, lack of interest, perhaps they don't like you... yet maybe they're not picking up because their phone fell in the toilet.

I tried calling one gentleman for months until I finally got ahold of him, and he was thankful that I called because he told me that his phone actually fell out of a three-story building and he lost everyone's information. Then he told me that he was so busy because his father was recently in a severe car accident. It wasn't long after that I was speaking before his team, too.

"You called so many times I thought it was an emergency."

I can't emphasize enough to Use Common Sense when being persistent. Be careful not to listen to the negative self-talk; however, be really aware of your thoughts so that you can master this. It's a fine balancing act.

You have to know enough about your business to know if you should make several attempts a day, a week, a month, and so on. It's different calling business to business. Often they are in sales and they may have more respect for your persistent attitude than a consumer who doesn't 'get it.' Use Common Sense but don't let your self-talk keep you from being persistent.

Understand that persistent doesn't necessarily mean call three times a day or even once a day. Persistent could mean call every three or six months for years. Although it *could* mean call once or twice a day. You'll have to be the judge of that.

Just recently I called a man two or three times in one day. He was a lead that was given to me, so the value of that is something I can use as leverage. "Bob highly recommends this program and suggested that I call you personally."

He finally picked up and said, "I saw you called several times and I see you're calling again so I picked up because I thought maybe it was an emergency." My response, "Oh, I'm so sorry. I just couldn't reach you, let me let you go and I'll try you later, no worries."

I backed off for about three days. I must admit before getting ready to call him the self-talk was definitely there. "Are you kidding me, Gary? You're really going to call this guy back after that?" That's the self-talk that you must not obey. I called him and he was the friendliest person and booked me right then and there on that call. Go figure!

When you think like this you will have story after story of people you ended up doing business with because you consciously chose to ignore your negative self-talk and *Voila!* You got the deal. Keep in mind, if you start accumulating stories like this, you, too – like me and Babe Ruth – will accumulate strikes and stories of people who were bothered by you even after only one or two calls. You can't have the good without the bad, but knowing how to make sure the good outweighs the bad is what you're learning here.

Buyer Beware: You Can Have Too Many Leads
A number of years ago I was speaking to the sales manager of a company that was sharing with me how his sales process works and how his team gets leads. He was in the copy machine business. He told me that each sales person has to get 25 leads a day when they are out and about in their territory.

Let's take a moment to think this through. 25 leads a day is 125 leads a week. So in a month they are required to have 625 leads. How in the world is one person going to follow up with 625 leads a month? That's absurd. It's not possible for one person to personally follow up with 625 leads a month and be very effective.

One day someone in my office called me up to tell me that just an hour away from him there is a convention with over 20,000 people. It's a market that we've been working for years. He wanted to know what my thoughts were about going there.

20,000 people at one location. It seems like a dream come true. But, after thinking about it, I chose not to waste our time going. That's right. I deemed it a waste of time. Here is why.

I looked at the leads we had. If we are to use our principle of 100 x 10 and we're having a challenge making that happen and regularly following up on what we already have, why add more leads to the equation? It doesn't make sense. "But Gary," one might reason, "20,000 people, come on. Are you kidding? Get your butt over there!"

If we had gone and gotten more leads here is what the numbers would start looking like. We would go from calling leads 100 x 10 to 200 x 9 to 300 x 8... to 800 x 3 to 900 x 2, and finally, you guessed it, 1000 x 1. How's that working for you? That would be what? Say it with me... STUPID!

Do you see the wisdom in *not* going to that event? We would have ended up with too many leads. Now it goes without saying that we can always hire more people to work more leads. Yes, that is very true, but at that time doing so wasn't part of our model. So we would have spent more time baiting the hooks and throwing in the lines than actually catching the fish.

Another reason going to this event might have *seemed* like a great idea for us is because we might have had too many mental barnacles on the ship already, and boy it would be so much nicer to start off with a whole new clean hull and start from scratch. It's the course of least resistance. Though a course like this appeals to our lazy human nature, it won't appeal to our wallet. Be smart at this game and you will win.

Chapter Six
The Mindset of True Persistence

When I talk about being persistent, understand that I'm not referring to using the same technique or tactic over and over again to try to attain a sale or a client. Never forget that being persistent has many facets to it. You must create and find as many facets as you can. Doing this helps you create an effective marketing campaign.

I believe you'll be much more successful in your sales if you look at every lead you have and include them as part of a marketing campaign. Calling someone once and throwing away their number is not what I consider a marketing campaign. To create a marketing campaign with your leads takes belief and vision. Let me share with you numerous ways to being persistent. I encourage you to use my ideas to help you get your creative juices flowing so you can think outside the box more than you ever have.

A Penny Compounded is Worth Millions; Your Efforts Can Be, Too
Perhaps you have had someone ask you the following trick question: "Would you rather have $10,000 per day for 30 days or a penny that doubled in value every day for 30 days?"

Being that I have forewarned you it was a trick question, you may have concluded to take the penny deal. Investors know to choose the doubling penny, because at the end of 30 days, we'd have about $5 million versus the $300,000 we'd have if we chose $10,000 per day.

Don't believe me? Let's look at this in detail. I'm sitting with a calculator and will give you a play-by-play in benchmarks.

On the first day, of course we'd have a penny. On the second day, we'd have two pennies. Then four, then eight, then 16. That's after five days. By day 10, we would have $5.12. It seems to start off a little slow, but be patient. We've gotten to the dollar values pretty quickly. By day 15, halfway through the month, we would have $163.84. The next part is where the magic happens.

By day 20, we have $5,242.88. Day 25? $167,772.16. Day 30 puts us at a whopping $5,368,709.12. Well over five million dollars.

This is why compound interest is often called the eighth wonder of the world, because it's so powerful. I want you to understand that your efforts in being persistent will work the same way if applied correctly. As long as you come at it from different angles, your efforts will eventually compound into results if you don't give up.

When you think one idea isn't working, be of the mindset that it's okay as long as your strategies include other facets. Don't focus on just one. When I refer to our 100 x 10 principle, it doesn't necessarily mean those 10 things have to be phone calls. It could be three calls, a thank you card, a gift, a personal visit. Be creative with this.

Something else that I use from time to time is I'll text a cute animal picture. I have one with a really adorable pug puppy that has the cutest, most innocent look as if he's saying, "Why are you ignoring me?" So I'll text that with a message. I also have an app where I can customize a caption personalizing it with their name. I actually have about 70 pictures on my phone like this. It changes things up and gets them to smile. This is priceless because the first thing people will subconsciously remember about you is how you made them feel.

Keep trying different facets and understand that if you keep dripping. sooner or later your efforts will compound. In order to achieve these results you must have patience, strategies, relentless persistence, belief, value, and vision, to name a few. You should also have the ability to see the big picture no matter how bad it gets or what others say about you in the smaller picture.

Cost is an Issue Only in the Absence of Value

Much of successful selling is based on a belief that I'm sure you may have heard before. Cost is an issue only in the absence of value. Let's think about this statement for a moment. If you call or meet someone face to face and they don't buy, ultimately the reason is that, for them, there is an absence of value. Sometimes you control this, but many other times you may have nothing to do with controlling it, as I'll be discussing with you shortly.

There can be endless reasons why this might be. Many times you might not be able to find out. It could be something as simple as stress. Someone could be so stressed out at the moment you call them that they'll have no interest in your offer because something else is pressing for their attention. You could be giving them a million dollars, but because they're so stressed or distracted, they may not have heard a word you said and gave you the cold shoulder with a no – or worse yet, a hang up.

So in this particular case, timing is the problem. Here is the wisdom in being smart, as we discussed in an earlier chapter.

You can't give up and you must keep the 100 x 10 going.

If you contacted someone and the timing was bad which resulted in an absence of value, why would you not consider making contact again later in the day, week, month, or year?

Peoples' circumstances change all the time. If you have a marketing campaign fueled by your vision of success you'll understand that, sooner or later, if you're in front of the potential customer more than your competitor, they'll take the bait with you first in many cases.

In order to create interest, we must present value. Don't think conventionally when you try to think of ways to present value. This is the time to think outside the box.

Transferring Value

Transferring value is one such technique and by far has been one of my most effective ways to remove the absence of value challenge. Here is how it works. A potential customer may blow you off because they don't see value. But if they had a close friend or a fellow colleague who used your product or services and respected the value in your offer, their opinion could change immediately.

Here is a scenario for you. I call a company CEO to make a pitch about seeing what I can do to get into speaking for one of their larger events. I make the first call and get blown off. Don't forget that ultimately he didn't show interest at the time because of the absence of value.

Now what do I do. First, I think. Here are the thoughts that go through my head: "Ok, he didn't give me the time of day. There was no possible way I would have even had the chance of giving him enough reasons to get him to see the value of my offer or work. What will I need to do to get to him so that there is no absence of value?"

And this is how I think and start the process. But I obviously don't stop here. I now must come up with answers within my marketing campaign. There are several possibilities. First, make contact within the corporation and get someone else to see the value in my offer or services and then get them to 'transfer' the value to the CEO.

Another way to do this is to find a leader within his organization that conducts their own meetings on a smaller scale that might be more open to allowing me in to speak for their group and then let that feedback get to the CEO. As you can see this becomes a well-thought-out campaign and strategy.

So then my team would search the name of a leader within the organization and make contact with them. I would even offer to fly in on my own dime and do training for the leadership team… but under one condition. I would be very up-front with the leader and let him know that we tried to make contact with the CEO with no success. I would tell the leader that I have a selfish motive to coming in to speak on top of helping his team grow. The selfish motive is to get testimonials from those in attendance and directly mail the feedback to the CEO. This is the ultimate goal in transferring value.

It's one of the most effective tools I know and use. After my presentation, I pass out little pieces of paper (nothing fancy) to all in attendance and I tell them exactly why I'm asking them to do this.

And after I have that feedback in hand, I mail them to the CEO. Before mailing them, though, I will scan through them.

If I happen to get the CEO's email, I send it that way later as well. Remember, sometimes you have to go through the front door, other times through the sewer, mail box, chimney, or wherever else, you name it. I can assure you that if the CEO gets ahold of just one of those testimonials, his perception of value will immediately start to increase. You'll have no idea how much, but even if it's just a little, it is progress.

I've sent some CEOs testimonials from their colleagues time and time again over the period of a year. I don't stop. How can someone fault me for having so much belief in what I do that I'm willing to travel the country on my dime to get in front of some of their team and prove my worth with more than just my talk, but with results from the field?

Always look for ways to transfer value. Keep thinking outside of the box. And when you think you've come up with more answers, stop and think of more. For example, I've taken pictures of some of the best testimonials and then texted them to a CEO if I have their number. If you stay in front of them, sooner or later their circumstances will change and you will want to be the person or company in front of them.

In one case, I called and texted for three years without a response. I made it a goal to fly to the city and stop by unannounced as we marketed to other companies in the same city. I dropped off some testimonials from local companies that he would have been familiar with.

The next day, I received a call from his assistant. The day after that, a 30-minute appointment turned into a one hour and forty-minute one. A month later, I was meeting most of the entire company's key players and executives. Three years of compounded efforts finally got results. Due to all of my relentless efforts I could write several books with stories like this. You want to be so persistent with such a strong belief and vision that you can relate success after success. If you can't, it's time to get moving. If you can, then congrats! ... And it's still time to get moving.

Kill Them with This & End Up with Class
Let me interject one very important point here that I've touched on in an earlier chapter. I cannot emphasize enough how important it is to kill them with a stupid amount of kindness.

No matter how nasty or rude someone is to you, you must kill them with kindness.

I had shared with you that if you're not this kind of person, then fake it at first. Yes, act this way even though you don't feel it. If you buy into this philosophy even if you don't like it, you will learn to be kinder if you make hundreds of calls or contacts. The reason is that, sooner or later, you'll see the results from it and it only makes sense to treat people this way.

I'll be the first to tell you that I'm not always Mr. Kind. I'm human, like everyone. But one thing being an incredibly persistent and relentless person has done for me is help me appreciate what someone like you and I have to go through on a day to day basis to become successful in selling. It's tough and challenging. It forced me to simply be as kind as possible to people no matter how they responded. It works and it keeps you in check when you make so many attempts to succeed in sales. You'll not only learn to *be* kind but you'll *become* kind. This also helps eliminate the barnacles and the emotional drag that attaches to us mentally with all the no's we get.

I recently had a manager of mine share with me a story about something that happened when he was training a new sales person. He was listening in on a call when the new person made a mistake and accidently insulted the potential customer. The sales person didn't realize what he had done till after he said it. The lady on the other end immediately hung up on him. Here is what our team is trained to do immediately when someone hangs up on them. Can you guess what it is? If you said call back, you are absolutely correct.

My manager did just that. The moment the lady picked up the phone, he immediately and sincerely apologized with kindness. She was amazed that someone would take the time to actually call back after being hung up on. This does several things. First, it immediately shocks the person in many cases, which often causes them to feel bad that they hung up and they are prone to listen to your apology. Second, most of the time we end up turning them around because we've got the belief and guts to call back with kindness. And third, whether they become a customer of ours or not, there is usually one word they commend us with for calling back with the positive, kind attitude we call with. The word is, 'class.' "You guys have class," is what we often hear.

Now imagine that. Instead of creating a story after being hung up on and bad mouthing the person, you instantly call them back, kindly apologize, turn things around, and they wrap up the call by referring to you and your company as someone with class. Want to have more class? Try this on for size.

Here is another way to have a potential customer end up thinking of you as having class or simply having more respect for you. Let's say you have exhausted all angles and you finally get in contact with whom you need to and you get that, "No!" They tell you they have no desire to do business with you. Now what? Do the classy thing. Send them a thank you card saying, "Thanks for taking my call or meeting with me. I do appreciate that as I know you're busy." I can assure you, they'll *never* forget you. In fact, I've found the ruder they are to me the more they remember me after sending a card like that because they just can't imagine someone taking a time out to do something like that. Try it!

Here is something that recently happened to me. I received a referral from a customer and I called the referral several times. When someone gives me a referral of someone they respect and know well, I will often make a few more attempts than normal because of the transferring of value.

This gentleman finally answered and began to tell me why

he wasn't interested and then the phone went *click*. So what are you supposed to do when that happens? Not curse at them but yes, call them back immediately. And I did. He didn't pick up, so I left a message that went like this: "Hey Bob, this is Gary again. I'm not sure if you hung up on me (said with a very friendly and respectful tone) or one of us are in a bad spot and the call got dropped, but please try me back again and I'll do the same. Thank you kindly for your time and I look forward to chatting again soon."

It's very important to make sure you use the right tone and it's got to be one of kindness, not rudeness or sarcasm, especially when you get to saying the words, "hung up on me." Well, lo and behold, take a guess who called me back the next day. He sure did. Of course he denied hanging up on me, but I'm okay with that. I wanted to continue with the dialog. These are the kind of results you can have when you have the guts of a burglar. And boy can it change the dynamics of how you presently do things.

Relay – Let Someone Else Do the Work for You
In aviation we have a term that we refer to as getting or offering a 'relay.' I'll give you an example of how it works and how it's used. A number of decades ago, before GPS was made readily available, I made a flight from Florida to Jamaica where I was born and raised. My uncle was interested in purchasing a single engine high-performance aircraft. I told him about one at the local airport. After speaking with the owner, he wanted me to rent the plane and fly it down for him to look at it.

He suggested at the time of the flight that I not try to go through the hassles of flying over Cuba and all the red tape that was involved in that at the time. The other alternative was to fly around it, which adds up to an additional three hours or more and a lot more time flying a single engine plane over the water.

As I flew out over the ocean for hundreds of miles, eventually the air traffic controllers were no longer able to maintain radio contact with me. It can be a very empty feeling, knowing that you have no one to talk to in case of an emergency. Not to mention this was my first and longest flight ever over the ocean. I didn't have lots of experience so my stress level was pretty high.

So to let the air traffic controllers know my position and location, I would relay a message to a commercial airliner 30,000 feet above me because my airplane was too far over the ocean and at too low of an altitude to be picked up.

I would hear an airliner speak to an air traffic controller. Then I would call the airliner and it went something like this.

Me: "Air Jamaica Six, Yankee, Juliet, Mike, Pappa this is November one, two, three; how do you read."

Commercial airliner: "November one, two, three this is Air Jamaica Six, Yankee, Juliet, Mike, Pappa, loud and clear go ahead."

Me: "Could you please do a relay for me?"

Commercial airliner: "Go ahead with the relay."

Me: "Please tell Miami control that November one, two, three is approximately 100 miles north, northeast of Haiti and expected to land to refuel there in about 40 minutes."

And that's pretty much how it goes. So the airliner contacts the controller on your behalf because, for whatever reason, you're unable to.

So I thought over the years, if that worked for us pilots why can't I use a similar approach in sales? If you're doing business to business especially, how often do you try to get to the decision maker but can't because of a gatekeeper or the person is never available for whatever reason? The following is how my relay would go.

Me: "Hey Betty. I've been unsuccessful for some time in trying to get ahold of John. I was wondering if you would kindly print an email that I would like to send you and then I'll try you back in the next hour or so to see if this is something he's willing to meet with me about. I only need five minutes or less with him on the phone. Okay?"

In this relay I'm pretty much telling her as opposed to asking her to help me out. Just go into the conversation with the assumption that he or she will help you out. I can't begin to tell you how many people I've gotten through by relaying. It's very creative and very effective.

There is a slight drawback from time to time using the relay. In a sense, you're somewhat relying on someone to do a mini-sales pitch for you and if they blow it you could be toast. But I'd rather attempt the relay as a last resort than walk away not making contact at all. Even if you get a no, it's better than being in a holding pattern. If I get a no and I think the potential customer is worth pursuing (100 x 10), I'll devise another strategy to continue with.

Let Go if You're Too Emotionally Attached

I shared earlier with you the importance of not creating a story or a negative association toward making repeated contacts. This – as I think you'll agree – is not the easiest thing to do. After years of pursuing a contact, there are times that I get a bit sick and tired of making more calls to the same company year after year. I don't like to admit that, but it's true and I'm human. So instead of tossing the lead away, I hand it over to someone else.

It's easy for someone else to call on your behalf because they don't have the years of making the phone calls like you do. To someone else, it's a brand new lead… a totally clean slate.

Then, after they've tried for a few weeks or months, they can give it back to you. If the lead is worthwhile, this is worth doing. Don't let your negative emotional attachment toward the lead cause you to dismiss it, especially if it's a whale.

Your stories will always creep up. It's that self-talk that none of us can totally control all of the time. What we *can* control is whether we choose to obey the self-talk or not.

Chapter Seven
Lay Down the Law: "You can't handle the truth!"

Here is a strategy that is very effective, but many people have a difficult time applying this one. You'll soon see why. If you can get over the mental hurdle that comes with what I'm about to share with you, you'll get to a yes or a no a lot faster.

The scenario here is you've called a person several times and are no longer able to contact them. We're assuming that contact had been made at least one time with what you thought might be possible interest.

Here is the message you might consider leaving, and in a very kind tone, of course:

"Hello Bob, Gary Coxe here. I've been quite unsuccessful in making contact with you again. I know you're busy but am also not sure if you've even been getting my messages. Could you at least give me the courtesy of letting me know if you're interested in continuing our conversation by texting or leaving me a message? This way I won't be wasting both of our time. Thanks so much. Chat soon."

This message is very effective and does several things. If they are truly interested I'll often get a phone call back with an apology from them. "Oh yes Gary, we'll still interested but timing has been terrible." And then you can continue to work toward the close. But at least now you have something to go on.

Often if they are not interested they usually won't call you back or text you, but some do. I find sales people have a problem leaving a message like this because they are afraid of getting that no. *They can't handle the truth.* I personally would rather leave a message like this and get the no now instead of wasting my efforts and getting the no weeks or months later. At least if I get a no I can figure out what my next plan might be. Try it. Lay down the law and tell it like it is. You'll be surprised how many people will respect you for being so frank with them, provided you left the message in a professional and kind tone.

Find a Mole (It's an Ethical Bribe)

In movies and espionage jargon, a mole has access to secret intelligence and subsequently works his way in to the target. You're not looking for secret intelligence but you are trying to work your way to a target who is a decision maker. Maybe you can find a mole in a company to help you out.

Pharmaceutical companies do this all the time, not to mention they spend millions and millions of dollars doing it. They'll spend money on lavish dinners and lunches or golf outings for the receptionists to get to the doctors who make the decisions. I obviously don't recommend doing something like this as an unethical bribery. Some companies have strict rules about things like this and you do want to respect them or someone could get fired, not to mention you won't get the sale.

There are a number of companies that I know of who have people within their organization willing to help me contact their CEOs or other leaders. If they're willing to help you, try to do something in kind for them.

Then there is the person who is a social butterfly who knows just about everyone.

Never forget that it's often not *what* you know but *who* you know, or who knows whom.

It's not uncommon for me to find someone who is well-connected and offer to pay them thousands of dollars just to meet certain people; a bonus if the meeting converts into a sale within a specific period of time.

Be careful about offering money without results. It's often best to pay for results and have them help you get in the door and work the lead for you if they have any influence on your potential contacts. This is thinking outside the box. If your sales don't result in high enough dollars then offer to pay accordingly. Maybe you can offer a free trip, tickets to a game, or dinner at a nice restaurant.

This is just another way to be creative.

I gave one lady nearly $2,500 worth of my programs to help me connect with some leads. It goes without saying she truly believed in what I had to offer. The deal, though, was that she personally had to call the people on my behalf with a recommendation and then follow up again if we couldn't get through in time. Make these deals clear and specific. My return on this investment paid off handsomely.

I've had people offer to help me without wanting a thing in return. If I get a large sale through the efforts of their help I will surprise them with a gift of some kind. The more you give, the more people are willing to help.

You might be surprised if someone helped get you a lead which converted into a sale who wasn't expecting anything from you. If you send them a gift card or cash, how much more they are willing to help you in the future? People do crazy things for cash. Cash is king!

Try finding a mole and see what happens. They can do things for you that you can't do yourself and they can shave months or years off of getting you to a contact. The cost of what you offer them to help you may often end up being a savings compared to the amount of time you'd have to invest in getting connected yourself. Not to mention the increased sales.

Tag Team Them

Keep in mind that not every strategy can be used for every person. Everyone has a different sales model or approach. If one doesn't fit yours, at least allow it to get your creative juices flowing to see what other ideas you can come up with from brainstorming with me as we go over these ideas together.

Sometimes you have come from several angles, and to do that, it takes two or more people. This just amounts to two people calling the same person. Of course you have to balance how often the calls are made. Don't make it seem as if you're attacking them. You'll say something like this if leaving a message: "Hello John, I understand you've been chatting with one of my colleagues, Betty. I was just checking in to see...." It's a friendly, non-intrusive approach.

This has several benefits. Like people often attract. You might have to swallow your pride and accept that your contact might like your colleague more than you, or vice versa for that matter. Why lose a deal because of pride? You'll have to determine how you split the commissions but if you want to increase your sales and have more fun, think outside the box more than you do now.

Let's be honest. Maybe you've tried to get an appointment with someone whom you've attached such a story to that you've allowed it to beat you up mentally. You may have too many negative associations attached to this potential client and every time you call you can't shake it off. Give it to someone else who doesn't know the difference. It will be fresh to them. Then later you might want to take it over again.

I have people that will only take my calls after my team has tried and tried. On the other hand, I have people who happen to take a call from one of my team members and not me initially. Put your pride away and figure out what it's going to take to get the deal. Tag teaming them might be the answer.

A Cute Text Never Hurts

With today's technology and smart phones you can do a lot with text messaging. There are many times I'll attempt to text a person knowing I have the right number and they refuse to text me back. To get their attention, I send them a cute picture with a caption. There are many apps you can search that will do this for you. It takes about 30 seconds. I alluded to this a little earlier, but let me go into more detail.

I found a picture with a guy who fell asleep with a baby colt. It's an adorable picture. After several unsuccessful attempts to call, I'll text this picture with a caption using their name that reads, "So Bill, are you saying we're not a good match?" This tactic does several things. First and foremost it shows you have a sense of humor. And second it helps break their pattern of thinking, "Oh no, not this guy again." At the very least they might say it with a smile.

I have another picture of a huge Saint Bernard laying down with a toddler in a diaper hugging the dog. I'll text this picture with the same caption as well. I have a collection of about 70 or more pictures that I got from the internet, saved to my desktop, and emailed them to my phone. One Sunday afternoon I spent about two hours hunting down funny pictures that I thought I could attach a fun message to.

I found one of a large bit pull with a sign hanging from its neck that reads, "My owner will be back soon." With a little bit of graphic magic I removed the words in the sign so that I could add my own custom caption.

I might add something like, "Sue, I know you're busy, but could you throw Gary a bone and take a call? :)" I often use a smiley face to make sure they know I'm having fun.

I recall using a 'mole' who had a meeting with a CEO that I had been contacting regularly. I asked him if he would put in a good word for me when he saw the CEO. He said he would have no problem doing that. I told him I'd send him a text as a friendly reminder if he didn't mind, being that I knew he had more important things on his plate.

This lets them know you appreciate that they are busy and you're willing do to the work and be the reminder. I then needed to determine what picture I would text when the time came. I recalled taking a picture a month earlier of a groundhog who was standing on his hind legs with his front feet under his chin. With a simple program, I placed a sign under his front feet to make it look like he was holding it and added the caption, "Hey Ray, don't forget me tonight! Thanks! :)" I texted that about an hour before he was to meet my contact. He responded immediately and put in a good word for me shortly after that.

I can't emphasize enough that being relentlessly persistent can be fun if you are creative. I love sending fun texts with captions and pictures to see what kind of response I get. It puts the fun back into selling. You could even make a personal video that's very short and text that. This is also a very effective means of communicating with your contacts.

Mail Them Something Cool and Different

I did a little survey on a social site where I asked people to vote on what flavor pudding they liked. The choices were vanilla or chocolate. Chocolate won, hands down. For over ten years we've been mailing everything from postcards to ad specialties to many of our whale leads. This time we sent over 100 chocolate puddings with about 10 very strong testimonials. I included a spoon and a napkin as well. I added a simple letter that read, "The proof is in the pudding." That was it. Need I say more? I had a business card placed in the box as well.

Never forget that one of these ideas may not entirely do the trick, but it all compounds. So don't get discouraged if you don't get immediate results. If you are in this for the long haul you will compound your efforts and get results.

During some campaigns I send something out every two or three weeks and do this for up to a year or more at a time. One of my millionaire mentors made some of his fortune in the specialty advertising business. His name was Dan Bagley. I met him when I was the ripe age of about seventeen. He would always emphasize the importance of ad specialty marketing.

For example, I've sent out flashlights with my website on them and a letter that read:

Without proper light we're all in the dark. Fortunately, there's a way to shed light on increasing the size of your organization and getting those new recruits to stay in the business which results in increased sales and profits.

As a service to your industry, I have taken my decades of experience and packed them into a FREE report on 'Five

Dangerous Trends Affecting Your Industry that STOP Growth and Profitability.' It's yours for free!

As you know, over 90% of those who start up fall by the wayside. That's a huge financial loss.

YOU'RE LOSING MONEY RIGHT NOW!

Don't get caught in the dark as to why this happens. This FREE report gives you the answers. Call NOW to shed even more light on these trends. (Add phone number)

To your continued success,

Gary

Let's discuss this letter. Note that it is very short and to the point. It always reminds them of the pain that they are experiencing. In this particular case it's the loss of income due to an enormously low retention rate. I'm offering the solution to help fix that and the longer they take to respond, the more money they lose. I give them the pain and offer the solution to relieve the pain. Keep it simple and about them, not YOU! To the correct receiver of this letter, I'm offering lots of value. The late author and sales trainer Chet Holmes does a really good job with this kind of marketing. He encourages having a long-term, tenacious attitude.

I send small screwdrivers in the mail. I go online and look for ad specialties on clearance and purchase hundreds of items to get a discount. Mail out stress balls with a heading like, "Stressed out about losing money in a challenging economy?" Expose the pain you have the solution to alleviate. I could go on and on with the many ideas I've used in past years. There was a really fun one we did many years ago when I was doing lots of TV shows about reversing people's fears and phobias to demonstrate how quickly change can be made. One of our goals was to get more media coverage and we needed to get the attention of TV producers.

So we purchased small boxes, about 3" x 2", with a cover. We poked holes in the box and placed custom stickers on the box that read, "Live Animal – Open with Caution." Of course there were no live animals in the box. It was part of the marketing. The holes where punched in the box to give the appearance that there was a live animal inside and it needed to breathe.

In each box we placed a picture of a tarantula. And boy did we get their attention! Just about every producer we called took our call. Granted this marketing is a bit extreme, but you have to admit it was very creative.

If you don't have a vision and you're not relentlessly persistent, you will get results that reflect that.

The key to all of these ideas is don't stop. Success doesn't happen overnight. Dive into this for the long haul. If you go into this with that kind of mindset, you look for things to do over a long period of time. There is no giving up because you're going to be at this for years to come. If you're not going to be, you efforts will give away that you're not.

Be Smarter with Your Advertising Budget

I once met a gentleman who had purchased an airplane that he was using for charting executives. I asked how he advertised his services. His marketing plan was simple yet genius. When we think about budgeting advertising dollars for different kinds of advertising, the most common methods often come to mind. Billboards, online ads, pay-per-click, newspapers, brochures, flyers, magazines, and so on. His advertising budget was a little smarter, more creative, and *very* targeted, not to mention highly effective.

Here is how he would spend his dollars. To a very targeted, prequalified group, he would offer his aircraft for charter at no cost. That's right, absolutely free. Here is his reasoning. Let's say his cost round trip for an executive charter was $1,500. He said he would get a much higher return spending that $1,500 on a free trip with highly qualified clients with a strong chance of them returning as paid customers than a one-time ad in a magazine for the same cost. I think that's brilliant and I've used this principle many times over.

If you're selling a product or service, why not consider taking your advertising dollars and, instead of using them for conventional advertising or in conjunction with it, take those dollars and purchase more of your product to give away. Let them see, feel, and touch what it is you have to offer. Then continue with your follow-up process. You might find this much more effective than simply paying for advertising.

Here is how I took this idea and made tens of thousands of dollars. When I started my "Beyond First Class" program where you fly with me in a private jet as I whisk you away to one of my events, a private island, or backstage to a TV show, I wanted to get the word out. To operate a private jet is very expensive. I thought about advertising this in magazines and through other means. But using the idea I just shared from that gentleman, I hit a home run many times.

Instead of advertising this program in a magazine and paying thousands of dollars for it, I offered the publishers of the magazines I was interested in a free trip to see what the experience was like – if they in turn would be interested in doing an article about the adventure. This amounts to giving away a 'free' seat in the jet and losing income with the hopes of a return on the investment from readers of the magazine once the story came out.

So either way I'm out a couple of grand. Either pay for an ad or use up a seat and fill it with a publisher of a magazine willing to do a story. Not to mention a story in a magazine has much more pull and credibility than an ad.

Well, it worked. After the "Beyond First Class" adventure from the Bahamas was over and the article came out, I got two phone calls. One gave me a deposit for over $14,000 over the phone with a credit card.

A story in a magazine has much more pull and credibility than an ad.

There was yet another example where I invited an influential leader of a company on one of my next trips. It was designed to build a relationship with him and his organization. It worked out great. The word spread and I ended up with more business into the six figures and a great friendship.

If you've gotten anything from this chapter I hope it's how to look for more creative ways to be more persistent and market yourself smarter. Push yourself to really think outside the box and know what that truly means. It means to look for the most unconventional ways to get in through the front door, the sewer, the mail box, the chimney, or by whatever means you need to. You must not give up. If you keep your eye on the ultimate goal of making contact with a decision maker then you don't stop until it happens. If you know there is gold six feet underneath you and your start digging and your shovel breaks, do you stop? Of course not! You gnaw through the dirt with your fingernails if you have to. You won't stop until you figure out a way to make things happen.

The more you think like this, the more creative you'll become. You'll be amazed how creative you can be when the words, "quit," or, "give up," don't exist as an alternative plan. When you have this kind of a mindset, you think and function on a totally different plane.

Acknowledge Your Persistence

Be prepared to acknowledge your persistence. Let me explain this further. I know right off the bat I'm persistent when approaching a company. If I make a phone call and get through to my contact I'll often say something like this, "Bob, bear with me as I learn to be more persistent than passive. You can be assured that I'll stay in touch. I don't mean to bother you or keep calling but I know you're busy and aren't always the easiest person to contact."

Just a simple acknowledgment like that opens up the door to keep following through. I'll often leave a voice message like this as well. "I know you're busy. I'll keep trying and hopefully call again when the timing might be better for you." With a little chuckle and a very friendly voice, I'll conclude with, "Bear with me!" You'd be surprised how that takes the wind out of their sails.

I'll wrap up with a perfect example of this. Have you ever seen those reality TV shows with people locked up in prison? It is absolutely amazing to me how unbelievably creative these inmates are. Because they are bored but have goals, they find a way to make and do things with extremely limited resources. They are forced into a mindset that makes their creative juices flow.

I've seen them create knives — "shanks," as inmates call them — from plastic. Cut metal bars with dental floss. Make instruments to tattoo themselves. One inmate showed the camera how he made and fermented his own wine. All this in his own prison cell. They made necessity the mother of invention.

It's time that you make sure you do the same. Make the necessity of contacting someone and converting the nibble to a catch force you to come up with creative ways to get results. If you make this mindset a must, you'll be blown away with creative ways to get through the door and watch your sales soar. All of this will happen because you now know that *You Can't Fillet a Nibble...* you can only fillet the catch!

About the Author

Personal Growth Expert and Life Strategist Gary Coxe is recognized for his life changing programs. His goal is to help others live an extraordinary life through lasting change. Gary is the author of the book, DON'T LET OTHERS RENT SPACE IN YOUR HEAD and others. His work has been seen on everything from *The View, Inside Edition, Fox and Friends,* regularly featured on CNBC's The Big Idea with Donny Deutsch, Oprah's program, The Nate Berkus Show, Success magazine, Selling Power, and numerous other national newspapers and magazines. NBC alone has spent over one million dollars producing his TV segments.

Gary started his first business at age 11 and a second at age 17; he was soon making over $100,000 a year as a teenager. After being mentored by two millionaires and later a billionaire, his life took a very unfortunate twist. He lost everything from his family to his wealth, all by age 21. He is truly a graduate of the school of hard knocks and is not afraid to admit it. His tragedies have given him an incredible ability to show people how to make dramatic change in their lives.

He has successfully broken through all of these limitations and much more. Today, individuals, athletes, CEOs, and corporations seek Gary out to share with them his techniques on how to peak at their highest level possible. Whether it is to increase their sales, their potential, or any block that limits their success, he demonstrates how to change negative cycles of thinking to positive, programmed conditioning.

Gary does not consider himself a motivational speaker, even though he is a powerful motivator. He feels that people don't want to get pumped up for just a short time. He believes they want to learn how to stay pumped for life. This, in turn, gives them the desire and motivation to keep stretching to higher levels. It is Gary's earnest desire to teach others to condition themselves for ultimate success as he travels the world sharing his self-mastery techniques. Learn more at www.garycoxe.com or call 1-800-64-POWER.